Shall the Circle Be Unbroken?

Helping the Emotionally Maltreated Child

Marilyn Franzen Holm

Library of Congress Card Catalog Number 85-072741
ISBN 0-917665-09-0 (cloth)
ISBN 0-917665-15-5 (paper)

Published in 1986 in the United States of America by
Bookmakers Guild, Inc.
1430 Florida Avenue, Suite 202
Longmont, Colorado 80501

Printed and bound in the United States of America

This book is dedicated to my husband
and to everyone else who works
to see the circle broken

Contents

The Most Deadly Sin

Some day, maybe, there will exist a well-informed, well-considered and yet fervent public conviction that the most deadly of all possible sins is the mutilation of a *child's spirit*: for such mutiliation undercuts the life principle of *trust*, without which every human act, may it feel ever so good, and seem ever so right, is prone to perversion by destructive forms of consciousness.

—*Erik Erikson*

Preface

Another book on child abuse? Another grisly account of beatings, burnings, chokings and other perversions inflicted on children by parents and others? What more can be said?

My experiences as a social worker, teacher, foster parent and mother of three have convinced me that the way we are treated as small children is, by and large, the way we treat ourselves the rest of our lives. In my work I have seen, too, that people from the poorest, least educated of mothers to the most eminent, erudite of professionals can impose agonizing torment upon themselves. For many it is difficult, perhaps impossible, to escape in later life the inner suffering imposed in childhood by adults, some sadistic, some well-meaning.

Maybe the pain was so brief and so insignificant we are largely unconscious of it. Maybe that pain is the factor most profoundly affecting our lives. This book sets out not to titillate with stories of physical abuse, but to explain how the humiliation, rejection and lovelessness suffered by many people to one degree or another in childhood affect our later lives.

The consequences of emotional maltreatment of children are rather simple: the effects on one individual are passed down to new victims. The Bible speaks of the sins of the fathers being visited even to the third and fourth generations. Today we may refer to that phenomenon as the circle of abuse. Shall the circle be unbroken? Shall we continue to pay the enormous costs related to emotional abuse?

No easy answers exist to solving the problem. Before we can find the answer, we must ask many good questions. Only through knowledge far greater than what we now possess will the intergenerational circle of misery be broken and children be given the opportunity to grow up loved and accepted.

Few books are solely the effort of the author, and this one is no exception. My special thanks to Dr. James Kedro, who had the confidence in me to propose it; thanks too to Dr. Fred Lindberg, Dr. Kent Christensen, Lois Distad, Jean Dawson, Carol Baum, and the many children whose true stories fill these pages. Details have often been changed to protect their privacy but the essential facts have not.

Thanks especially to my family—Steve, Erik, Katie and John—who uncomplainingly put up with my neglect of them through the research and writing of the book.

Introduction

As I glanced through an observation window to see how the visit was going, the scene etched itself forever into my memory. A small boy—his thin frame and blond head putting me in mind of my own son—huddled in a corner. Over him towered two adults who were shaking their fists in his face. Words like rocks were flying at the boy. "It's your fault, you miserable little bastard."

In ten seconds, I'd seen and heard enough to interrupt the visit by entering the room and changing the subject. The child looked at me with an expression of immeasurable gratitude.

The facts I knew were these: The mother and father had put their son in foster care the previous month, saying he was obnoxious and uncontrollable. They wanted him "out of their hair." Because this little boy appeared to be at risk for abuse, he was placed in another home as social workers tried to figure out what to do about the situation. It hadn't been my case, but the foster mother whom I supervised called frequently to ask questions and to report on what was happening with little Michael.

"He wants so much to talk to his mom and dad," she'd tell me. "But they never call him; I don't know why. He's an angel! He makes my own boys look bad!"

I reminded her that many foster children can maintain good behavior for a time we call "the honeymoon" and asked her to keep a diary while

Michael stayed with them. When the agreed-upon month had gone by, Michael's parents were finally told they must have a visit with their son, that they couldn't just park him with a child welfare agency and walk away. The time was set, and Michael's social worker was scheduled to observe the visit. Just before I happened to walk down the hall and routinely check what was happening in the visiting room, she had been called away.

It was hard for me to control my anger at what I saw through the window—two large adults ganging up on a sobbing six-year-old. Without knowing many of the details, it seemed obvious that Michael was being emotionally abused.

Because of the interaction I'd observed, the parents met with me and other workers later that day. It came as no surprise that they weren't ready to take Michael home. His mother hinted that she might not want him back. Ever.

We tried to determine the reasons for the parents' rejection. "He's always been a troublemaker," the mother said. "Always." When asked to give an example, the parents talked about Michael throwing up at the table after every meal from the time he was two.

"He does it on purpose!" the father slammed his fist down on the table. "He does it because he knows it will make me angry."

"And he's so disobedient," the mother added. "He gets into food when he's been told a thousand times to only eat at meals. I've found packages he's opened, the sneaky little thing!" The look in her eyes was one of cold fury.

It didn't take long to see that the parents had totally unrealistic expectations for a six-year-old. I wondered about the fearful emotional climate existing in the home that caused a child to frequently vomit at the table.

Several months earlier, a complaint of physical abuse had been made against the parents. A concerned neighbor had noticed bruises on the child and questioned Michael. As is often the case, Michael denied to him the beating he had received for having left his bedroom to go to the bathroom. The neighbor had not believed Michael's story and had gone ahead with his complaint.

When questioned, Michael's father readily admitted the belt-beating he'd given, saying his son had to learn to obey. "That's what's wrong with this country," he'd said. "Parents don't discipline their kids anymore."

During the investigation, Michael was upset and blamed himself for being the cause of the questions. After his parents were advised to use less severe punishments in the future, Michael was returned home.

The parent–child relationship, never good, had gone downhill from that time. The child's father was convinced the boy had deliberately tried to make his parents look bad, and he was shut in his room for hours at a time with food slipped in through the door. If he got off the bed or made any noise, he was told to expect worse than he'd known before. A pet kitten, choosing a bad time to meow, was thrown against a wall and her neck broken by Michael's father as the frightened boy looked on. "Remember the kitten," would be enough to keep Michael silent for hours at a time after that incident.

Deplorable details of Michael's life with his parents began to emerge from the diary kept by his foster mother. She repeated a story Michael related—one that had no "explanation," just the facts as a small boy might present them.

"I was lying in bed one night when Mom came in my room. She had the butcher knife in her hand. She sat down beside me and tested the knife against her finger to see if it was real sharp. Then she put the point in my throat."

Probably reacting to the look on his foster mother's face, he hurried to explain that he hadn't been hurt. "She just kind of laid it here," pointing to the hollow in his throat. "But the next morning when I woke up, there was blood all over my hands."

The sinister meaning of the incident has never been unraveled.

The chronicle of emotional abuse Michael had been subjected to could go on and on. The workers involved became convinced that this was not an isolated incident of child abuse. These were no parents who out of stress or ignorance had punished their child excessively. Instead, they seemed determined to treat Michael with a calculated rejection that only meant one thing. They did not want him in their lives.

When confronted about the pattern of rejecting behaviors shown to their son, the parents admitted they did not want him. Papers for relinquishment of parental rights were drawn up and signed by them. At that time, the parents asked to have no more to do with Michael, leaving any explanation to their son of what had happened as the social worker's responsibility.

"Sorry," they were told. "You must explain to Michael yourself about the relinquishment. Michael would never believe a social worker who told him you didn't want him. But this time you can tell him that what's happening isn't his fault."

The foster mother brought Michael back to the office the day of this last visit. With tears in her eyes, she escorted him to the visiting room where the parents waited. She knew how desperately Michael was hoping that today would be the day he'd go back home to be with his own parents. Like me, she knew this wouldn't happen.

"Sit down, we have something to tell you," Michael's mother said. "You aren't coming home with us today. Not today or ever. You're going to get a new mom and dad. Someone will adopt you."

The sound that came from Michael—part sob, part wail—was the saddest sound I've ever heard. That cry from a small, abandoned boy seemed to echo the pain, anguish and hopelessness of abused children everywhere. The sight of Michael's body wracked with a silent crying filled my eyes with tears.

Maybe because Michael is an unusually winsome child, maybe because I identified him with my own small son who is so dearly loved—whatever the reason, I couldn't forget about him. I kept wondering why Michael's parents treated him as they did, and why the topics of emotional abuse and neglect are largely ignored by professionals. I wrote a column about Michael for the local newspaper and was surprised at the reaction it received. Partly because of that column this book came about.

In researching this book, I discovered that since 1961, when the American Academy of Pediatrics began focusing attention on battered children, most definitions of child abuse have given only passing notice to emotional abuse. In practice it is rare, indeed, that cases of emotional maltreatment are diagnosed, let alone treated, by professionals. Nearly always, when the emotional maltreatment of children is addressed, it is because physical and/or sexual abuse has also occurred. This is frustrating to me because abuse is not an isolated physical/sexual trauma, but a syndrome of pathological parent-child interaction that causes devastation to the child.

As I read medical, legal and social work journals in preparation for writing this book, I began to understand why this is the case. Mental health professionals have largely avoided the topic because it is so elusive and at the same time, so devastating. At the present time it's nearly impossible to objectively decide what parental behavior constitutes abuse, except perhaps for the most visible, extreme cases. What is abuse to one person is "loving discipline" to another, and neglect which kills children is waved away by some as merely being due to cultural or lifestyle differences. From Biblical times to the present, advice on raising children has varied and changes with the times. Rigidity gives way to permissiveness that, in turn, is made obsolete by some newer approach.

The purpose of this book is to explore problems of definition, but more importantly, to urge progress in dealing with the emotional maltreatment of children. For despite difficulties in defining emotional maltreatment, it *does* exist, and in the opinion of many professionals, is the root of most other forms of abuse. With or without accompanying physical and sexual maltreatment, the costs to individual children and society, as a whole, are overwhelming. This book is concerned with the enormously destructive effects of emotional abuse and neglect, and it suggests changes to help break the vicious circle that grinds through generation after generation of unhappy parents and children. And it is a vicious circle, because the family of our childhood is, for each of us, the source of unconscious design for later life. If, like Michael's mother, a person's earliest experiences are ones that tear down self-esteem or, even worse, never build it, the pattern has been formed for the grown child's family. When emotional maltreatment—whether neglect or abuse—occurs, the damage is not limited to the momentary victim. The painful conflicts in the child, the inability to trust, love and act in competent ways, shape the personality in a way that spirals unmercifully into the next generation.

For those who, by virtue of having grown up with love and respect or the right genetic background, consider themselves "good parents," sections on raising emotionally healthy children and helping adults feel good about themselves are included.

Because, you see, this book is written for all those who believe the survival of humanity as we know it depends less on missiles and treaties than on the way our children are nurtured.

Chapter One

Why Would Anyone Hurt a Child?

The Antecedents of Child Abuse

The woman was aghast at what she'd heard about a recent case of child abuse. "Why would anyone want to abuse a child?" she asked me. "I just don't understand. How can parents hurt their children? They should be taken out and shot!" she said. We talked a little, then she became thoughtful. "What causes child abuse, anyway?" the woman inquired.

It was a good question, but unfortunately, not one that can be readily answered. Probably the best we can do is to define some antecedents for abuse, keeping in mind that what is considered child abuse depends on historical, cultural, legal and other judgments.

Child abuse is not a new problem. A history of violence against children can be traced back to Biblical times. The Old Testament dictum, "Spare the rod and spoil the child," has been used in support of brutality from ancient days to the present. Infanticide, castration and other forms of mutilation were perfectly legal for parents from ancient Rome through our own colonial period.

Social historians have chronicled a panoramic horror of the abuses that have been inflicted on children throughout the ages, in some cultures beginning at birth. Because the contemporary religious and political forces advocated such violence, one could probably make a case for the cause of today's child abuse being rooted in our institutional past.

1

Dr. Alice Miller, in *For Your Own Good,* translates an eighteenth-century German essay on the instruction of children. "Thus, after one has driven out willfulness as a result of one's first labors with children, the chief goal of one's further labors must be obedience. It is not very easy, however, to implant obedience in children. It is quite natural for the child's soul to want to have a will of its own, and things that are not done correctly in the first two years will be difficult to rectify thereafter. One of the advantages of these early years is that then force and compulsion can be used. Over the years, children forget everything that happened to them in early childhood. *If their wills can be broken at this time, they will never remember afterwards that they had a will, and for this very reason the severity that is required will not have any serious consequences* [italics mine]." [1]

The arrival of the Puritans coincides with the first recording of what we would call child abuse in America. "Beating the devil" out of a child then was not only an expression, but something many parents earnestly tried to achieve. Shunning, taunting, dunking and public humiliation were common disciplines for even very young children considered to be "saucy" or "headstrong."

Parents were given near *carte blanche* to kill their children who were considered beyond their control. These measures, along with such treatment as placing children in stocks, were justified as being in the best interests of the children because such discipline led them to salvation. Because many religious and judicial authorities encouraged such cruelty to children, the identification of child abuse for what it is was delayed for centuries. A member of the American Humane Society pointed out to me the irony of the fact that a society for the prevention of cruelty to animals existed long before its counterpart for children was formed. Even then, one hundred years passed before child abuse began to receive real recognition, and even at that only the physical manifestation of the problem was addressed initially. Truly, for centuries the world's children have been the targets for the anger, frustrations, projections and unmet needs of the adults who presumably were to be their guardians and protectors.

It was not until 1962 when Dr. C. Henry Kempe and his associates published their classic, "The Battered Child Syndrome," in the *Journal of the American Medical Association* that physical abuse began to be scrutinized. However, by the end of that decade, all fifty states were sufficiently aware of the problem to enact legislation dealing with abuse.

Physical abuses must be addressed because, while no psychological trauma is created by accidental bodily injuries on the part of the parents, the assault is harmful. It says that the adults to whom the child looks for protection and warmth are unreliable and hurtful. Neglect tells the child he is worthless and nonexistent. Unfortunately, the emotional maltreatment of children that underlies physical abuse has only recently begun receiving attention. However, damage to the young spirit does not result from bodily harm so much as from the emotional maltreatment underlying it. Unless emotional maltreatment is considered as basic to the problem, efforts to heal or protect the child are doomed to failure.

During the past twenty years a great deal of research has gone on to determine the cause of child abuse. If the cause or causes could be found, the problem could presumably be eradicated by vaccine. People's behavior is infinitely more complex than bacteria, however, and most of the "reasons" for maltreatment that have been advanced have been found woefully simplistic. For example, we have not been able to consistently and accurately predict the occurrence of child abuse. With our current knowledge base, the best we can do is to describe usual antecedents for abuse. They are sometimes grouped as follows: the personality or psychiatric model, the social-situational model, and the ecological model.

THE PERSONALITY MODEL

"There's got to be something wrong with a person who'd hurt a child," according to many people who hear about an abuse incident. That perception—defective personality as the root cause of maltreatment—was probably the first attempt at explanation. According to the defective personality theory, psychopathology, mental illness, drug or alcohol abuse, for example, lead to maltreatment. Dr. Henry Kempe has estimated, however, that less than ten percent of child abusers can be classified as being mentally ill.[2] Even allowing for this conservative estimate, the defective personality theory is obviously an insufficient explanation of the roots of most abuse. At the same time people whose personalities have been twisted and thwarted by maltreatment are much more likely to be abusive and neglectful.

The idea that parents are always right and that every act of cruelty, physical or emotional, is somehow an expression of their love, is deeply implanted in people. Because that idea is based on a process of internalization that takes place during the first year of life, during the period that precedes a baby's conscious awareness that she and her parent are not the same person, the conviction is ingrained that cruelty is not the parents' fault, but is due to some quality or shortcoming in the child. Although parents always mistreat their children for psychological reasons (attempting to meet their own needs), there runs deep the idea that this treatment is good for children. Alice Miller graphically describes the "whole gamut of ingenious measures applied 'for the child's own good' which are difficult for a child to comprehend and which, for that very reason, often have devastating effects on later life." In *For Your Own Good* she explains, "This is where the difference lies between treating an adult and a child cruelly. The self has not yet sufficiently developed for a child to retain the memory of it or of the feelings it arouses. The knowledge that you were beaten and that this, as your parents tell you, was for your own good may well be retained . . . but the suffering caused by the way you were mistreated will remain unconscious and will later prevent you from emphathizing with others. This is why battered children grow up to be mothers and fathers who beat their own offspring; from their own ranks are recruited the most reliable executioners, concentration-camp supervisors, prison guards and torturers. They beat, mistreat and torture out of an inner compulsion to repeat their own history and they are able to do this without the slightest feeling of sympathy for their victims because they have identified totally with the aggressive side of their psyche. These people were beaten and humiliated themselves at such an early age that it was never possible for them to experience consciously the helpless, battered child they once were. In order to do this, they would have needed the aid of an understanding, supportive adult, and no such person was available."[3]

Have any personality characteristics of abusive/neglectful parents been identified? Although many studies have been made, no coherent, "causative" portrait has been drawn. The only general agreement appears to be that abusive parents express aggression inappropriately. No consensus exists, nor have reasons for this behavior been found.

SOCIAL-SITUATIONAL MODEL

R. J. Gelles has pointed out that the personal problems which the personality theory attributes to causing child maltreatment arise from social antecedents such as marital conflict, unemployment, isolation and other stresses. He proposes that neglect and abuse arise when inadequate resources for parents are combined with approval of non-nurturing methods of childrearing.[4] This approach focuses on both the immediate context that includes the parents and child, and the larger social environment. This environment can include all people and events which affect the parent-child relationships. Interpretations of intent ("The baby is trying to make me mad"), disposition ("She's been hard to manage since she was born"), and negative feelings about personal child care abilities ("I'm a rotten mother") would belong in the immediate context. Some of the likely interactions leading to these three perceptions include feeding, dressing, toilet training or the child's exploration activities.

A thorough study of child-abusing mothers matched to non-abusive controls found several characteristic differences. Abusive mothers tend to accept child abuse as a part of parenting, to hold grossly unrealistic expectations for children, to see them as intentionally bad, and to have a history of abuse or neglect in their own childhoods.[5]

Grossly unrealistic expectations for children have been mentioned by several researchers. Consider the following:

"Abusive parents misperceive age-appropriate behavior as willful disobedience. Crying is often interpreted as critical and accusatory . . . those behaviors of the child which do not fit with the parents' wishes are ignored or misinterpreted."[6]

". . . when the child fails to perform properly, the parents attribute this behavior to deliberate stubbornness, willful disobedience or a malicious desire to thwart their wishes. In the parents' style of childrearing, such behavior, of course, calls for severe punishment."[7]

These are the parents who describe a baby as "out to get me" or as "wanting to make me look bad." The abused child is seen as purposefully malicious and having the knowledge and ability to bring about their abuse or, as one mother told me, "She asks for it."

Such perceptions by the parents of the child's intentionally "misbehaving" and being "bad" are obviously damaging to the developing parent-child relationship. Just as you would be more angry if you believed a waiter deliberately dropped food into your lap than if you believed the spill was an accident, so parents who believe that their children—even infants—are intentionally messy or soil their diapers are more apt to respond aggressively. Another way that this intentionality damages parent-child interactions is by preventing parents from considering the real causes of behavior. The child's crying, for example, may indicate not that he is "out to get" the parent, but that he's hungry, tired, in pain or reacting to parental harshness. When the parents project the crying as the child is acting bad or greedy, they feel justified in doing nothing (neglect) or punishing (abuse). When parents who have injured babies for crying express their motives, it becomes obvious that they saw their child as defiant, attacking, or depriving them of their basic needs such as sleep or freedom.

Other infant/child behaviors that elicit hostility from the parent and can be considered "intentional" are thumbsucking ("trying to act like a baby"), biting ("being mean"), turning away or refusing to eat ("disobedience"), and not going to sleep ("rebellion").

Many researchers have found that along with attributing intentionality and disposition to infants and small children, abusive/neglectful parents have lower self-esteem than control groups. Abusive mothers studied tended to express far more self-criticism and anger than control mothers. Remarks such as "I felt like I was losing my mind because of the baby" or "I didn't know what to do. I just wanted to let him cry till he couldn't cry anymore", reveal the depression, helplessness and potential for abuse or neglect by these mothers.[8] One psychologist has theorized that abusive parents experience their child's disobedience as a threat to their own deficient self-esteem, which triggers anger and aggression toward the child.

Ronald Rohner has described social factors that thwart healthy parental attachment. Mothers the world over, he has discovered, are likely to reject their children if they are unable to get away from time to time, at least briefly. Neglectful and abusive parents tend to expect little from others in the way of friendship or support, trying to avoid rejection and anger by breaking off close personal ties. Sometimes they avoid caring relationships with neighbors, friends, co-workers or even family. If both parents feel isolated and over-stressed, the family will have no outside sources of support at these times. Family members are then required to meet all family needs, setting up a strong likelihood for abuse.

Often the potential abuser becomes an actual abuser during stressful times. Dr. Rohner found that in those households where an alternate caregiver (support) is available to help assume child care duties, the atmosphere was likely to be more safe and affectionate than in those households where the parent is given no relief. (This assumes assistance cheerfully given. Dr. Rohner notes wryly that "forced" fatherhood, or a parent who stays at home because of unemployment, does not count as support.)[9]

ADOLESCENT MOTHERS

Often unmarried teenage mothers are considered to be more apt to abuse their children. According to the social-situational model, when inadequate financial, emotional, and care-supportive resources are combined with approved non-nurturing methods of child rearing, such as inconsistent and often uninformed practices, the likelihood of abuse by adolescent mothers increases. This possibility has been investigated by many researchers.

Although experts have compiled strong evidence associating children's delayed cognitive development with adolescent mothers, they have not built as strong a case implicating young mothers with a higher incidence of abuse. While samples are small, studies available do suggest that the younger the parent, the higher the risk of abuse. Not surprisingly, research indicates that those variables associated with parents who have a high risk of abusing their children are the very factors commonly found among teenage mothers. The pregnancies are likely to be unplanned, and the child is raised by a single parent. S. F. Hartley has found that children born to unmarried mothers are three and one-half times more likely to be victims of child abuse than children who are born legitimately.[10]

Because physically and mentally handicapped children are more often born to adolescent mothers, statistics reveal that handicapped children are frequently abused by their mothers. The reason for this may be that, for a mature mother, the task of providing for a child with cerebral palsy, for example can be formidable, but for a mother in her early or middle teens, the stress would probably be overwhelming.

A review of the literature suggests that although maternal age seems to be associated with the developmental progress of children, other variables such as "psychological, social and demographic factors seem to be more critical determinants . . . many of these mothers have motivations and attitudes that are psychologically questionable concerning the bearing and raising of children."[11]

In summary, although many problems are described, a careful examination of research to date does not clearly implicate adolescent motherhood *per se* as leading to child abuse.

What of poverty? Has it been established as a cause of maltreatment? While B. F. Steele and C. B. Pollack and many others have found physical abuse of children to be more common among the poorer classes,[12] recent observers suggest that this is not the case with emotional maltreatment. Contemporary lifestyle has produced children raised from infancy in day care, children who then become latchkey kids, who often are victims of affluent neglect.

CHILDREN AS BURDENS

Richard Logan has proposed that today's children are often considered hindrances by parents dedicated to self-fulfillment. If certain types of abuse or neglect are attributable to living in poverty, the other side of that problem is the status of *burdens* that many well-off children occupy.[13] Dr. Lee Salk, in a speech to parents in Minneapolis, raised the hackles of some feminists and working mothers by suggesting that a child needs a full-time parent during the first three years of life. (He concedes this parent is usually the mother.) It is during the child's first three years, he believes, that it is most important to know that someone really cares, cares enough to stay home and spend time with him. Without a full-time (or nearly full-time) parental caretaker, the child will think of himself as a burden, someone who "gets in the way," according to Salk. Although children may grow up with no visible scars from years spent in day care or with babysitters, the child psychologist believes that they often feel deeply that their parents would be better off without them.

In the past, in tradition-oriented societies, slow-changing village or agricultural groups, children were valued as continuers of tradition. They were expected to have, and usually held, unquestioning acceptance of their roles. They were economically needed and took on important labor responsibilities early in life. During these times, children, especially girls, received many years of training as a future parent. They were often responsible not only for brothers and sisters, but also for the extended family's children. Children in a tradition-oriented society grew up learning responsibility and feeling valued because of these contributions to the larger society. In fact, as historians have pointed out, the notion of "childhood" as a separate and special age of life has come to be universally accepted only during the last two centuries. Prior to that, children were not considered significantly different from adults. They were thought to be merely smaller and somewhat inferior to adults. (This was not believed true of infants but of children six or older.)

As this "old" society changed to today's urban, industrialized, "new" society, the family unit was greatly affected. An industrialized society required geographic mobility and so the nuclear family came into its own, as jobs requiring moves away from parents and aunts and uncles came into existence.

Now, when the nuclear family is cut off from the older generation, the members tend to look more to their contemporaries rather than their elders for direction and values. The nuclear family society becomes "here and now" oriented.

As ties from generation to generation weaken in such a society, ties to contemporaries become much more important, and the society tends to segment, separated from other age groups. Today we have a "youth culture" and "retirement communities," entities that would have been unthinkable a century or two ago.

Instead of having learned to confidently raise children within the family, most new parents today must turn to "experts" and how-to books. Most of today's young parents don't live close enough to grandparents or other kin to benefit from their support and advice.

Along with this separation of young parents from the older generation, came a separation of children from the world of real work. Part of the reason for that change was the abuse of children by unhealthy and unsafe labor practices. Probably a more influential reason is that mechanization replaced the unskilled labor of children and teenagers until they were no longer needed for work. When masses of those displaced poor children began filling the streets of Europe in the nineteenth century, governments began compulsory education laws. In addition to several other effects, compulsory education further served to isolate children from the larger society by physically and socially segregating them in school buildings.

Out of this segregation of children from work and responsibility, as well as from tradition, grew the perception that children are burdens. Dr. Bruno Bettelheim noted that parents rarely have a responsibility today to "pass on" their trades or life's work to children as a part of tradition. As a result, one of the oldest reasons to prize children has disappeared.[14] Children are seen as burdens when the parents begin to think of their children as consumers rather than producers. Perhaps part of the problem lies in the seduction of parents and children alike by modern advertising. Parents are convinced that they must supply more goods and services to meet their children's needs, while the children's expectations for goods and services keep growing at an astonishing rate. The stress of affluence keeps the parents working harder and harder (separated all day from other family members) to acquire more and more material comforts for their children. These unrealistic expectations often set up situations where abuse is likely to occur.

As young couples (who have been raised to expect more or less instant gratification of their material wishes) begin families, they often experience real conflict. They've heard advertising tell them repeatedly that they're number one, "worth it" and other egotistic themes. When they become parents, the new demands of child-rearing threaten the parents' possibility of uncontested self-fulfillment. A screaming baby takes precedence over a parent's search for meaning (or it should). To young people brought up in the religious pursuit of self-gratification, a seven-pound infant can create shock waves. Whose needs take precedence?

Even when planned and wanted, the child often becomes a hindrance. He grows up with unreasonable expectations for achievement in the middle-class world of his parents. The right climate for emotional abuse has been created.

ECOLOGICAL MODEL

The third, and possibly most satisfactory model, for explaining the complex nature of child abuse and neglect was proposed by James Garbarino. He examines maltreatment in terms of the relationships between three interacting systems. On the first level he explores the individual, including his developmental progress. The second level details the social interactions of marital and parent-child relationships, including conflicts, stresses and satisfactions. In the third level he examines the environment and asks what social supports and institutions exist that negatively or positively affect the other two levels.

Although the ecological model is somewhat complicated, it explains child abuse and neglect as follows: The child is at greatest risk when both the parents' and child's functions are characterized as being developmentally limited. At the second level of the model, if the relationship between spouses or between parents and child produces additional stress, the risk for abuse goes higher. If, at the third level, no supporting institutions or people exist in the community to help the beleaguered family, the risk climbs higher still. Not surprisingly, the rates of substantiated child abuse are highest in communities where few helping programs or agencies are available.

Each of these levels could be examined in detail. For the purpose of this book, however, the first level, that is the individual's developmental progress, seems to be crucial.

We start from the premise that a person's emotional development depends on the way his mother experienced his expression of needs during the first months of life. If a parent cannot take pleasure in the infant as he is, but must immediately begin setting up conditions for love, the foundations for rejection and depression have been set.[15]

In *Prisoners of Childhood* (an apt description of adults who become abusers and neglecters of children) Dr. Alice Miller states, "Many people suffer all their lives from (this) oppressive feeling of guilt, the sense of not having lived up to their parents' expectation. This feeling is stronger than any intellectual insight that it is not a child's duty or task to satisfy his parents' . . . needs."[16]

Many years ago it occurred to me that people often repeat some childhood experiences in their adult lives. While in graduate school, I learned this was hardly a unique insight on my part, but one that is basic to understanding much of human behavior. Each of us is "programmed" from early childhood to react in certain ways to certain types of situations. This "programming" is strong and enduring, and can be changed only with great effort. We recreate experiences—even harmful ones—because they are what we know. In examining the circle of child abuse, we see that while adults don't necessarily play the same roles they did as children, they tend to set up situations in which the same roles can be played out.

The background of abuse in their own childhoods emerges as the preeminent characteristic of parents who mistreat their children. B. F. Steele describes the unbroken circle.

"It is out of the pool of abused, neglected children that the next generation of abusive parents will come. These unfortunate people have carried into their adult life their main psychological patterns of lack of trust, fear of social contacts, inability to have pleasure, low self-esteem, mild depression, great neediness and inability to empathically love . . . when they have children they repeat the behavior of their own parents; they expect their children to behave in ways to satisfy the excessive parental needs. Especially in times of crisis the parents turn to their babies for comfort. The children are bound to fail and are punished or neglected. The cycle repeats itself." [17]

These unmet emotional needs are described as *Unfinished Business,* the title of a book by Maggie Scarf. She writes "In early childhood we haven't the capacity for repairing (or salving) our own psychological hurts and wounds. We aren't able to truly look within; to introspect and communicate with ourselves. In the preschool years we master anxieties and distress by dealing with them in play—that is, we play them out in games. Older children in the latency period (ages 6-12) deal with problems and difficulties by *not* dealing with them; in other words they try to avoid thinking about matters that may be painful or frightening—to keep busy with preoccupations of a variety of sorts." [18]

When a parent has grown up emotionally deprived, he searches throughout his life for what his own parents could not give him when he needed it—the presence of a person completely aware of him, a person who takes him seriously, who admires and follows him, someone who is "just crazy" about him.

This sad search can never be very successful because it really goes back to a time in early childhood when the self was being formed. Past traumatic experiences of rejection or humiliation have deformed present emotional responses. Victims are inadequately prepared to respond in healthy ways to everyday life or crisis situations, and often manipulate their environments to reenact their childhoods.

Susan, a woman who repeatedly abandoned her child, had learned as a small girl that the most appropriate objects for gratification are the parents' own children. She was never taken seriously by her parents, and when she became a mother, she craved from her child the respect she had never received from her parents.

Susan's ex-husband, who was seeking custody of the child, told me that Susan constantly talked about getting plastic surgery on her eyes, and within a short time after their marriage, insisted her husband never look at her. Convinced that he felt disgust and shame when he saw her, she permitted him to talk to her only from another room or at best while standing behind her. She eventually insisted on her husband wearing a paper bag over his head, which, unbelievably, he would do for hours at a time. From her child, however, she demanded an unflinching stare directly into her eyes, flying into verbally and physically abusive episodes when the little boy would finally break eye contact.

After hearing about and reading reports concerning her, it came as a surprise for me to meet an attractive woman with lovely, cornflower-blue eyes. What Susan thought others saw when they looked into her eyes is something about which Freudians might speculate. What was most upsetting for me was the aberrant behavior her six-year-old son was already showing. Was it too late to break the circle? The story of Susan and her son illustrates a parenting deficiency whereby abused children are used for the emotional gratification of parents without regard to the children's needs. These children grow up with the same emotional failures and keep the circle of misery grinding along.

ATTACHMENT BEHAVIOR RESEARCH

Harry Harlow probably has the distinction of having done the best-known nonhuman research on the causes of abuse. In 1957 at the University of Wisconsin, he began years of experimentation on attachment behaviors and the effects of maternal deprivation. Many readers might recall seeing pictures in psychology texts of Harlow's baby monkeys and their wire-frame "mothers," some with cloth covers, others with bottles for feeding.

One of Harlow's experiments on baby monkeys separated from their mothers was to pair them with a "rejecting mother" (also a cloth-covered wire frame apparatus.) This apparatus was constructed so that on schedule or demand it would abruptly hurl the clinging infant away from its "mother." Other experiments included among various rejecting behaviors, a "shaking mother" which at the experimenter's control would wildly jerk the infant around, and a "porcupine mother" which had brass spikes protruding over its front. The infant monkey in search of any physical contact with its "mother" was forced to crawl painfully over the spikes.

As these baby monkeys raised away from their natural mothers grew to maturity, they became increasingly deviant. They sat for hours without moving, staring blankly and remaining strangely silent. In the manner of autistic children, some covered their heads with both hands while rocking back and forth. Others were self-mutilating and required medical attention. Although all physical needs, such as food and shelter, had been satisfied, these baby rhesus monkeys had grown into profoundly disturbed adults.

When the unloved, abused female monkeys became mothers, the results were grim. Harlow described two characteristic behaviors of these unloved babies-turned-mothers. First, they totally ignored their babies, neglecting them to the point that death would have occurred without intervention. This response is completely at odds with the behavior of normally raised monkeys who attentively and tenderly care for their young.

In addition, these same mothers actively rejected their children; in what Harlow described as a "grim and ghastly" manner. "When the infant would make tentative contact with the mother's body, she would disattach the infant. She would literally scrape it from her body and abuse the infant by various sadistic devices. The mother would put the baby's face against the floor and rub it back and forth . . . in most cases, our experimenters were able to stop sadism at this point, but some mothers were so violent and so vicious that the baby was barely saved or even lost . . ." [19]

This research has implications for anyone interested in finding the causes of emotional abuse. Though criticized by some as being cruel, Harlow's experiments with monkeys have chillingly established the cyclical effects of lack of attachment. There are striking parallels between what Harlow's deprived monkeys teach us and the studies of small children described in the next chapter.

To return to James Garbarino's ecological model for explaining child maltreatment, we can see that if at the first level the individual mother or father has a history of being an abused or neglected child, *and* if this limitation is combined with conflict between spouses (second level), *and* if the support system in the community does not exist or does not effectively intervene (third level), the child is at high risk for maltreatment.

Chapter Two

What Grandma Always Knew

The Need for Attachment

Dr. Selma Fraiberg, a child psychiatrist, describes what would be the amazed reaction of her grandmother, if she were alive, to the recent findings of infant psychologists and researchers.

" 'Love begins in a mother's arms? Did someone just discover this?'

"She would be amused by the jargon we have invented to describe the process of mother-infant attachment. 'Tactile and kinesthetic stimulation.' 'Mutual gaze patterns.' 'Visual stimulus of the mother's face.'

"She would be pleased and not surprised to find her own maternal wisdom vindicated by contemporary science."[1] The facts that babies smile at their mothers' voices at four weeks, that they recognize and prefer mothers to others before six months of age, and that they do better when comforted than left to cry would not be news to Dr. Fraiberg's grandmother.

Yet some new ideas have emerged from the research of many scientists such as Rene Spitz, John Bowlby, and Selma Fraiberg. Thanks to the pioneering work of these individuals, we now know that "learning-to-love," or attachment, as it is called by professionals, is far more than just a side-effect of being fed. We have learned, in scientific fashion, that the human baby must experience the presence of a mother (or mother-substitute) for psychological survival. From studies of unfortunate babies who were institutionalized because of the death, disaster or indifference of their mothers, the importance of attachment became obvious. Researchers found that babies who were regularly fed and sheltered but not given the opportunity to attach or to learn-to-love showed astonishing and alarming mental and physical deficits.

Although the experts may disagree on some things, they do agree about the importance of beginnings. They agree that a child cannot grow up whole, separate and self-reliant unless someone has loved the baby enough to first give her a healthy self concept, then let go. That love begins at birth with the mother's touch, smile and gaze.

Recent studies reveal how incredible is the newborn's capacity for learning from the first moments of birth. The idea that children are born "blank slates" with little ability to sense or respond has been disproven. Very soon—during the first few days of life—the baby learns how to change her environment through reactions and behavior. She learns that a cry quickly brings someone to relieve distress, that a smile elicits delightful reactions from her mother. According to the type of reactions given by her parents, the baby may learn to be more aggressive and controlling, or perhaps more docile and loveable. Parent and child each shape the other.

Despite the insistence of pediatricians for years that early smiles are due to "gas," researchers have learned this is not the case. Although the smile that occurs when a baby is a few hours old is bestowed indiscriminately, it affects the parent–child relationship almost immediately. A smiling baby is a virtual advertisement for parenthood. The parent will almost always respond with smiling, babbling and cuddling. A sick or crabby baby may not draw the same type of positive reaction, making attachment of the child to parent more difficult to develop.

Drs. John Kennell and Marshall Klaus have defined the concept of attachment as "an affectionate bond between two individuals that endures through space and time and serves to join them emotionally." Sometimes referred to as "bonding," it is a *requirement* if the baby is to grow into an adult who has attained intellectual potential, who can think logically, and handle fear and anxiety. Attachment is a requirement, too, if the child is to develop a conscience, become self-reliant, be able to cope with frustration and control unacceptable behavior. The concept of attachment is crucial to understanding the cycle of abuse and neglect because the degree to which early attachment is present or absent profoundly affects the future ability to love and be loved.[2]

Although attachment research usually refers to the parent as mother, a new realization is growing about the role of fathers. The work of Dr. Ross Parke has dispelled some common myths about the father, including the one that he is inherently less competent than the mother to care for a baby.[3]

Dr. Parke has found that when left alone with the infant, the father is very sensitive and responsive to her needs. He believes that a high degree of involvement on the part of the father in daily caretaking and play leads to a strong infant-father bond. Furthermore, his research indicates that the child who grows up well-attached to both father and mother copes better in later life. According to Parke, children react better to the stress of being left alone with a stranger if their fathers are active and involved caretakers.

Other studies have shown that compared to children who are reared only by their mothers, preschoolers who also have attentive fathers tend to have higher self-esteem, higher satisfaction with their gender, higher achievement levels, and higher levels of social functioning both with children and adults.

Erik Erikson believes the function of the child's first year of life is to build trust and to become attached to her caretaker. As the infant comes to trust that her needs will be met, she will become attached. Erikson feels that a caregiver's love and care are absolutely essential to building a sense of trust and that the critical period for developing that attachment is during the first year. Necessary ingredients for normal attachment to occur are eye contact, feeding, smiling, and physical contact such as rocking, cuddling, and carrying.[4]

Dr. John Bowlby's name may not be a household word, but his findings of the last thirty years have greatly influenced the ways institutions and people treat babies and small children. Instead of believing "Let the baby cry; she'll get spoiled if you pick her up," most parents realize now that satisfied babies don't grow up to be spoiled, but rather contented. Children whose needs have been met are not the ones who grow up "spoiled" but rather those babies whose basic needs for comfort weren't heeded. Most experts today agree that comforting a crying baby will not spoil her. It will instead help her learn that her parents can be depended upon to help her.

It is to Dr. Bowlby's credit that in the Western world "orphanages" are largely a thing of the past, and children without families are placed with foster or adoptive homes whenever possible. It is because of Dr. Bowlby's work that hospitals no longer ban parental visits because the child will "settle down better" without parents around. Because of his work and that done by those who followed him, the parents of a premature child who must be kept hospitalized are encouraged to participate in feeding and other nurturing activities while the child is still hospitalized. The list could go on and on. Nurses, doctors, teachers, parents and social workers may never have read a word written by Dr. Bowlby, yet their attitudes and work have been greatly influenced by the ideas he put forth. Today it may be considered only common sense that children need mothers—something grandma knew—yet there was a time professionals and parents had lost sight of just how much babies really do need mothers, and what the dire consequences are should adequate attachment not occur.

Although Bowlby's basic premise goes far beyond implications for early childhood, his view that attachment and loss are the two poles of life experience implies that these issues strongly affect our entire lives. The need for intimacy and support, as well as the emotional upheaval from their absence, are concerns that stay with us to the grave.[5]

The attachment process is not something that the mother (or mother-substitute) "does" to the baby. It has been described as a ballet dance in which the mother and child respond to the steps of the other. If the mother feels good about herself and her baby, the baby will pick up the feelings and, by reaction, reward the mother. A circle of satisfaction and love is set in motion.

Fraiberg writes of the "love language" that the infant of less than six months possesses, a language that can be used to reward the mother. "There is the language of the embrace, the language of the eyes, the language of the smile, vocal communication for pleasure and distress. It is the essential vocabulary for love before we can speak of love. Eighteen years later, when this baby is full grown and "falls in love" for the first time, he will woo his partner through the language of the eyes, the language of the smile through the utterance of endearments and the joy of the embrace. In his declarations of love he will use such phrases as 'When I first looked into your eyes,' 'When you smiled at me,' 'When I held you in my arms.' And naturally, in this exalted state, he will believe he invented this love song." [6]

These delightful sensations are among those that occur during the process of attachment. As Fraiberg points out, they recur in adulthood when we "fall in love." That fall, in many ways, is a return to the dependency and vulnerability of the infant.

In the beginning, babies don't recognize or relate to the mother as a separate human being. Most anyone who provides necessary food or comfort is acceptable. Before six months or so, however, the special attachment to one or both parents usually becomes evident in psychologically healthy babies. Strong preference is shown for the mother—the baby smiles more for her, coos more for her, exchanges more glances and extends more eye contact, and will begin to follow on all fours if she leaves the room. Sometime around six months of age the baby will be unhappy if mother leaves. What this means is that the process of attachment is becoming well-established.

In most healthy babies, between six and nine months of age the discomfort the baby feels at separation from the mother can intensify and verge on panic. The child has no way of knowing that mother will soon return from the store or a weekend away with daddy. If for some reason, such as illness or death, the mother does not return shortly, the baby's grief can be overwhelming. Sleeplessness, apathy and loss of appetite, have been observed in babies who have no way of comprehending what has happened. As sad as this may be to see, the reaction of babies who have never known attachment is more distressing. A baby who has not attached to a mother or a father shows no sorrow at the absence of anyone. People are interchangeable, and no one has any special meaning or significance.

Sometime during the second year of life, according to Erikson, a basic position toward life is established, one that pretty much stays consistent into adulthood. If a baby's needs have been met consistently and warmly, he or she will consider the world a good and safe place. The baby will trust the mother, not only because she meets needs, but also because the mother conveys a sense of her own worthiness.

If the child's needs are not recognized or are met inconsistently, the basic life-position will become one of mistrust. A baby left alone and improperly cared for has no way of knowing that her parents are failing. Instead, she sees the world as harsh and unpredictable. A negative approach to life begins. Unless the circle is broken, this baby will grow up to be an unhappy, and probably irresponsible, adult and parent.

Sometime in the child's second year of life the infant who has formed a deep attachment to the mother begins moving toward independence and autonomy. "I can do it!" becomes the motto of the toddler who begins to explore the world in a steadily larger circle, occasionally returning to the mother for brief reassurance that she is still there. The child can handle short periods of separation better than at six months because mother has proved over and over that she will return. The healthy youngster, during the second year of life, has a well-developed sense of self, as separate from others, and a growing awareness that there are many people in the world. This child knows mother from father, sisters from brothers and is beginning to realize that people all treat him somewhat differently and seem to expect different things. Fear of strangers begins to fade.

Dr. Margaret Mahler, another prominent child psychiatrist, has extensively described the separation phase of the attachment process. Once the baby is able to creep and then to walk, he can take a role in determining closeness and distance to the mother. If the mother or mother-substitute is available (both psychologically and physically) when the baby needs closeness, the attachment process can proceed. Many times Dr. Mahler observed infants coming back to mother as "home base", touching her legs, leaning on her, or in other ways "emotionally refueling." "It is easy to observe how the wilting and fatigued infant 'perks up' in the shortest time, following such contact, after which he quickly goes on with his explorations, once again absorbed in pleasure at his own functioning." [7] The baby is well on the way to developing "personhood."

According to Dr. Mahler, as the toddler explores and begins trying to "conquer the world," a realization dawns that "the world is not his oyster; that he must cope with it more or less 'on his own,' very often as a relatively helpless, small and separate individual, unable to command relief or assistance merely by feeling the need for them or giving voice to that need." It is her belief that during this phase "the foundation for subsequent relatively stable mental health or borderline pathology is laid."

The implications of this statement are sobering. Misunderstanding and unrealistic expectations on the part of both mother and child often begin during this period. The mother may be baffled by the toddler's demand for nearly constant attention, especially since for a time she was not so demanding and, indeed, seemed determined to become independent. It seems contradictory to many mothers that while the baby is less helpless and dependent than six months earlier, she seems to demand more attention.

For some mothers, this is a frustrating time which sets the stage for abuse to occur.

Other mothers may enjoy the child's return to helplessness. They may unconsciously continue to keep the child dependent throughout her life by overprotectiveness, intrusiveness and "smother love."

Mahler believes strongly that the mother's continued emotional ability is essential during this stage if the child is to attain "optimal functional capacity. By the end of the second or beginning of the third year, the predictable emotional participation of the mother seems to facilitate the rich unfolding that is taking place in the toddler's thought processes, reality testing and coping behavior."

The word "bonding" is occasionally used to describe the attachment process as described by Bowlby, Mahler and others. It is not particularly helpful in understanding what happens in attachment since the word suggests a glued-on condition between parent and child. Actually, the process is dynamic, with periods of the child's withdrawal and self-absorption alternating with nearly complete concentration on the mother.

ATTACHMENT DISORDERS

What happens when the normal process of attachment as superficially described here goes awry? What disorders occur when developmental sequences of attachment are absent, disrupted or distorted? Child therapists and social workers can recognize such problems by comparing attachment behavior sequences shown or absent with those expected in a normal child of the same age. Excellent infant and child assessment tests are available for such evaluation of the developmental sequences of attachment (*See Table 1, pp. 24–26.*)

Most of the items from birth to eighteen months refer to the way in which attachment to mother develops. The items describing behaviors from eighteen to thirty-six months refer to ways the infant begins to free himself from earlier dependency. In emotionally healthy infants, the earlier attachments are maintained but modified by a growing capacity for independence.

By age three and a half, if the child has had a loving parent, he has a true sense of personhood—loved by mother and father, but with a separate life.

Table 1: Normal Attachment

Dr. Justin Call has described the normal behavior occurring in the developmental sequences of attachment for the child from birth to age three.[8]

1) <u>Birth to One Month</u>
   - The healthy newborn's attachment to breast, bottle and caretakers is dependent on several reflexes and movement patterns including rooting or head-turning response, sucking and swallowing reflexes. Very quickly the newborn's reflexes show the effects of learning; for example, hand-to-face contacts become increasingly directed and lead to hand and finger sucking. Crying becomes differentiated and by the time an infant is ten days old, many mothers can distinguish the child's hunger cry, for example, from other types of crying.
   - The healthy infant shows responsiveness and orientation to the mother's face, eyes and voice within a few hours after birth.
   - Attaching infants begin to show "anticipatory approach behavior" at feeding time as early as three days. That behavior refers to the baby's reaching toward the mother when placed in the feeding position before cheek or lips have been touched. Dr. Call notes that this "anticipatory approach behavior" is seen earlier in breastfed babies than those who are bottle-fed.
   - By three weeks when the attaching child is alert and attentive, he will smile at his mother's voice.
   - By three weeks he will imitate. Intriguing studies have shown babies younger than twelve days sticking out their tongues in response to researchers doing the same.

2) <u>One to Three Months</u>
   - Vocalization and gaze reciprocity are further elaborated. Mother and child take turns mimicking each other and enjoy playing the "cough game," peek-a-boo, and other play sequences.
   - When the infant realizes she is in a strange situation, increased clinging to the mother can be observed.
   - The infant begins to show "social smiles," especially for mother.

3) Four to Six Months
  ■ The infant can be briefly soothed by the mother's voice even when in moderate distress from hunger.
  ■ Spontaneous reaching for the mother occurs.
  ■ The infant postures for pick-up by mother.
  ■ Preference for the mother, as opposed to a stranger, intensifies.

4) Seven to Nine Months
  ■ All of the above attachment behaviors continue.
  ■ Expressive distress is shown (blank or worried face, crying, panic, crawling after mother) when the child is separated from the mother.

5) Ten to Fifteen Months
  ■ Above developments continue; in addition
  ■ The infant crawls or walks toward mother.
  ■ The infant demonstrates subtle facial expressions such as coyness, flirtatious interest, attentiveness.
  ■ Responsive dialogue with mother is clearly established.
  ■ Early imitating of mother's vocal inflections, facial expressions, hand and finger movements are observed.
  ■ Pointing gesture (extended forefinger) is used by infant in communication.
  ■ The child shows joy and relief when mother returns after separation, or, paradoxically, the child may show short-lived avoidance to protest or punish the mother for "desertion."

6) Sixteen to Twenty-Four Months
  ■ The child uses imitative jargon.
  ■ The child uses headshaking "no" gesture.
  ■ The child may use a "secondary transitional object"—a blanket or stuffed toy—in the mother's absence, especially at bedtime or when stressed.
  ■ Separation anxiety begins to diminish. Infant moves away from mother to explore, returning to the mother for sharing. (Mahler)
  ■ Infant finds missing or hidden objects.

7) Twenty-Five to Thirty-Six Months

- Child shows above attachment characteristics, plus
- Ability to tolerate separation from mother without distress when in familiar surroundings and when verbal reassurances are given about mother's return.
- Two- to three-word speech shown.
- Stranger anxiety is reduced.
- Object constancy is achieved. (The infant can maintain composure without regression in the absence of mother even during short periods of stress.)
- Social play with other children is enjoyed.

Separation is possible because the child doesn't have to worry about being abandoned or left defenseless. Erikson describes the child's first social achievement as "his willingness to let the mother out of sight without undue anxiety or rage because she has become an inner certainty." When applied to abused and neglected children who are compared to normal control group children, the deficits in their attachment processes become obvious. For them, mother has not "become an inner certainty."

EFFECTS OF ATTACHMENT DISORDERS

Three-year-old Jennie marched up to my front door with the social worker. When I opened the door, she put down her small suitcase and looked brightly around the room.

"This is Marilyn. She'll be your foster mother," the caseworker told Jennie.

"Hi, Mom," she chirped. "Where's your TV?" She breezed by me without a glance. My heart sank, because I guessed from her behavior that she was an unattached child. I wondered what had gone wrong in her infancy or toddlerhood, and what we as a foster family could do to help her.

Unfortunately, during those years we served as foster parents, Jennie was not the only child with attachment problems who was placed with us. Because of Jennie and the others like her, we learned firsthand how difficult treatment of these disorders can be, and how infinitely preferable is prevention to treatment. Given the potential long-term effects that attachment disorders can have on children, it is crucial that they be recognized and overcome as much as possible.

Bowlby, Fraiberg and others have written of the difficulties unattached children have in relating to others. Jennie, for example, showed lavish displays of affection—but only to anyone whom she considered a person who might do something for her. Already at three she had mastered coquetry that was devastating to every adult male with whom she came in contact. Her attempts to manipulate people were amusing, yet sad. When invited to our friends' homes for dinner, she would approach the woman of the house when I was in another room. "Can I call you Mom?" she'd ask, then relate a story of not having been fed all day. "So could I please have some ice cream right now?" she'd plead.

With older unattached children, we'd discover in addition to manipulativeness and lack of genuine affection for others, a total lack of conscience or remorse for wrongdoing. Sometimes in frustration I'd pound my pillow at night. "I give and give to this child. It doesn't seem to make any difference!" Intellectually I knew all the characteristics of unattached children, but living with one on a daily basis was still difficult.

How do these symptoms relate to attachment problems of infancy or early childhood? Remember, the baby's initial relationships with the mother or mother-substitute sets the tone for all future relationships. From her mother, Jennie learned she could expect nothing from others. She had not experienced a give-and-take with her mother, and from infancy she had approached people suspiciously and cynically, wondering how she could get them to meet her needs.

For various reasons—prolonged hospital care, frequent changes in caregivers, failure of the mother to develop patterns of attention and affection—children like Jennie do not develop a specific attachment to anyone. Later, they find it extremely difficult to build and maintain relationships that are anything but superficial. Because such children have not learned to love from their mothers and fathers, they continue living in that sad circle by not giving love to others. "What's in it for me?" is the attitude that determines most of their behavior.

Because children such as Jennie don't trust others, many behaviors are aimed at keeping people emotionally distant. If every adult woman is

"Mom", no one mother can be special or hurt the child by what she does or doesn't do. Some of the ways unattached children (and later, adults) keep others at a distance include:

Aggressiveness or Hyperactivity

Some children keep others away not only emotionally but physically as well, by biting, hitting, kicking or scratching. Children use these methods to avoid any demands on them. Many adults will choose asking nothing of the child rather than setting off aggressive tantrums. A child who seems to be "bouncing off the wall" from hyperactivity likewise keeps people at a distance. When the child is always on the move or easily distracted, intimacy is impossible.

Indiscriminate Affection

Unattached children can appear charmingly affectionate, disarming strangers with hugs and kisses. Although attached children may be very sociable with strangers, seldom will they act in the indiscriminately physical manner of many unattached children. Jennie, for example, would crawl up on the lap of any man who visited our home, clasping her little arms around his neck, saying, "I love you, mister." Often, even in small children, these interactions have a seductive quality to them.

Why would a child who has never known real love act like this? By her behavior Jennie was saying, "All people—especially men—are interchangeable. They can be manipulated into giving me things." She also managed to keep me feeling insecure and anxious since she appeared to give far more attention and affection to strangers than to her foster family.

Withdrawal

Many children who have attachment problems withdraw from others physically and/or emotionally. Some avoid eye contact and seem to literally shrink away from conversation or physical contact. Others may not avoid physical contact, but build an emotional barrier that doesn't permit real intimacy.

Over-Competency

One of the foster mothers whom I currently supervise called in consternation one day. "I just don't know how to handle Nancy," she said. "I can't do anything for her. In fact, I get the feeling she's trying to take over my place in the family!"

Six-year-old Nancy, a foster child, is an "over-competent child" in the jargon of social workers. Not only does she appear to not want or need a parent, but also as the foster mother reported, she eagerly seeks control. While a child who insists on doing a great number of chores around the house and assumes duties of child care, for example, sounds like the kind of kid every parent dreams of, it becomes unsettling to anyone who has lived with such a child.

Nancy was the oldest of several children who had been severely neglected by an alcoholic mother. This small girl had for some time done an incredible amount of household work, and had a fussy, "old womanish" quality about her. When the mother died, the children at first were placed together in a foster home as adoptive possibilities were explored. Because Nancy refused to give up her role as "mother" even then, she was separated for a short time and placed in a treatment foster home where the goal was to help her once again be a "little girl." It was a struggle to help Nancy reach the point where she could accept help and love when needed. Because of problems in attachment, the over-competent child's attitude is "I can get along just fine without you."

Lack of Self-Awareness

Donnie is the child my family will always remember because of his voracious appetite. As is often the case with children who have attachment disorders, his distress showed in eating habits. After eating at the table to the point of satiation, he would surreptitiously bring more food to his room where he'd eat to the point of vomiting. Repeatedly telling him he didn't need to hide food, that he could eat whenever he was hungry, had no effect on this behavior. Donnie seemed to have no awareness of real hunger or fullness, heat, cold or pain. Like many children with eating disorders, he was a bedwetter who didn't seem aware of any of the signals his body was sending.

Such behaviors often develop when a baby's needs were met infrequently or inconsistently. Many neglectful parents take care of their child according to their convenience or notions, rather than according to the bodily needs of the child. Therefore, the baby grows up without associating certain sensations and needs with appropriate relief.

Power Struggles

To be sure, battles for control can occur even in well-attached children. But the lack of trust found in children without good attachment leads to some power wars that can be titanic. The children constantly test limits set by authority figures. Even the most reasonable of requests by a parent can escalate into war. While it may appear that such children always want complete control, in reality they actually feel frightened if they can win. If a child can win in a power struggle, how weak must be the authority! More than anything, such children want firm boundaries and a sense of security that comes from knowing the parents are in control.

Lack of Conscience

Children with attachment problems seldom think twice about lying, stealing, or doing "sneaky" things. They may lie for what appears to be no earthly reason, about things that don't matter one way or another. One psychiatrist captured the attitude of a boy who was placed with us for some time. He said, "James believes 'What's mine is mine and what's yours is mine when I want it.'" Depending on the severity of the attachment disorder, such children may grow up sociopathic, unable to feel others' pain or joy.

Many other symptoms exist that indicate to professionals that somewhere in infancy or early childhood a problem in attachment occurred. They include a child being destructive to herself, to others, and to material things ("accident-prone"); a lack of impulse control; cruelty to animals; poor peer relationships; persistent and annoying nonsense remarks and chatter; preoccupation with fire, and excessive preoccupation with body functions or hypochondriacal symptoms.

Every one of us, well-attached or not, must work at finding a healthy balance between self-reliance or autonomy on the one hand and dependency or trust on the other. No one achieves this balance for all time. Instead, throughout our lives we swing between one pole or the other as changing circumstances and events affect our needs and responses.

Chapter Three

A Problem of Definition

Pinning Down Emotional Maltreatment

Imagine this scenario: a small girl huddles in her bed, listening for her father's footsteps in the hallway. Eventually he enters her room. "You have to do what I tell you or I'll leave home," he says. "You can keep our family together. But you mustn't tell your mother. She wouldn't understand our 'special secret.'"

In an emotionally austere family, this child, who is starved for attention of any kind, has been convinced she can keep her family intact by her acquiescence. Anxious, guilty, yet pleased by his intensity, she submits to the sexual advances of her father. Has she been physically, sexually, or emotionally violated?

The answer, all of the above, illustrates the difficulty in speaking of emotional maltreatment in isolation from other types of abuse. The coercive and manipulative climate in which sexual abuse takes place emotionally damages the child. Like all victims of emotional maltreatment, the child will come to believe that people are not worthy of trust, and that adults who should be nurturing givers are instead demanding takers.

Unfortunately, finding a definition that separates physical abuse from emotional maltreatment is only one of the problems in combating emotional maltreatment. The lack of consensus among experts as to what constitutes

33

emotional maltreatment and what should be done about it is discouraging. Goldstein, Freud, and Solnit, authors of *Beyond the Best Interests of the Child,* go so far as to deny any legal intervention for such grounds as "emotional harm" or "emotional neglect." They state, "These are too imprecise, in terms of definition, case, treatment and consequences, to ensure fair warning and thus adequate control over judges, lawyers, police, social workers and other participants in the child placement process."[1] They believe that even if emotional neglect could be precisely defined, "recognition of how little we know about the 'right treatment' precludes intervention." What should be done about children who are clearly emotionally maltreated by any sense of community and expert standards is not addressed.

Louise Armstrong comments in *The Home Front: Notes from the Family War Zone,* "Psychological abuse is scarcely definable and about as legislatable as bickering or withholding of affection."[2] Despite her sarcasm, a working definition of emotional abuse and neglect is crucial before significant progress can be made to break the circle.

Professionals are becoming increasingly aware that however it's defined, emotional maltreatment is the problem basic to all other abuse. There is growing recognition that abandonment, profound neglect, sexual abuse and all the rest occur secondary to that of emotional maltreatment. The "battered baby" syndrome cannot be understood or remedied without some conception of the emotional abuse and neglect that underlies physical abuse. The intergenerational circle of maltreatment and the "wounded child in the wounded parent" must be recognized and treated.

Most therapists and social workers who deal with abusive parents learn that their clients' backgrounds have these qualities in common: emotional deprivation, rejection, excessive demands and sense of unloveability. Contrary to what the general public believes, abusive parents were not always physically abused as children. However, emotional maltreatment was almost inevitably present in their histories.

For those who wish to see a perfect correlation between child abuse and later emotional illness, Alice Miller writes, "Those who swear by statistical studies . . . would have to be given proof that a given number of cases of child abuse later produced almost the same number of murderers. This proof cannot be provided, however, for the following reasons: Child abuse usually takes place in secret and often goes undetected. The child conceals and represses these experiences . . . Even if statistical data confirm my own conclusions, I do not consider them a reliable source because they are often either based on uncritical assumptions and ideas that are either meaningless (such as a 'sheltered childhood'), vague, [or] ambiguous ('received a lot of love') . . . My observations are lent scientific validity by the fact that they can be made repeatedly, can proceed with a minimum of theoretical assumptions and can be verified or refuted even by nonprofessionals."[3]

A well-known study of abusive parents conducted in the late 1960s found, without exception, "in our study group . . . there is a history of having been raised in the same style which they have recreated in the pattern of rearing their own children. Several had experienced severe abuse in the form of physical beatings from either mother or father; a few reported never having had a hand laid on them. *All had experienced, however, a sense of intensive, pervasive, continuous demand from their parents* [italics mine]."[4] Inevitably, the backgrounds of abusive parents are characterized by corrosive rejection and social deprivation.

One of the central issues in the definition of emotional abuse, then, is to understand the circumstances that lead to damage in the child. Much research remains before these circumstances can be confidently set forth.

An examination of some definitions put forth by various experts may illustrate the difficulty of pinning down just what constitutes emotional maltreatment. Referred to as mental injury, emotional abuse, psychological injury and many other labels, these forms of maltreatment have many common antecedents and effects.

The National Committee on Child Abuse and Neglect has defined mental injury as "an injury to the intellectual or psychological capacity of a child as evidenced by an observable and substantial impairment in his ability to function within his normal range of performance and behavior, with due regard to his culture."[5]

Another definition by Dr. James Garbarino states that "emotional abuse is the willful destruction or significant impairment of a child's competence."[6] He believes that "the most promising route for definition is to specify the meaning and implication of rejection, because it appears that rejection transcends culture. Broadly speaking, the definition of emotional maltreatment should revolve around the parents' rejection of the child's normal and naturally occurring behaviors that reflect the development of competence."

From the many definitions in the literature, these two exemplify the dual focus usually found. Condition of the child and parental fault are specified in a majority of the definitions.

As critics have noted, most definitions raise more questions than they settle. For example, take the following definition of emotional neglect: ". . . an act of omission, frequently the result of parental ignorance or indifference. As a result, the child is not given positive emotional support or stimulation. Parents may give adequate physical care to their child but leave him or her alone in a crib for long periods of time, seldom cuddle or talk to the child or fail to give him or her encouragement or recognition."[7]

Exactly what does this mean on a day-to-day basis in parent-child relationships? How often or profound need be the failure to "give him or her encouragement and recognition"? For a child protection agency to legally intervene, an operational definition setting forth specifics is needed.

What about intent? Garbarino's definition includes the word "willful." Does that make the child suffering from unintentional neglect less deserving of treatment?

Dr. Alayne Yates, a child psychiatrist, describes legal issues involved in definition. He notes that definitions of many states' statutes depend on observed parental behavior. "This entails the implicit assumption that the child's emotional state is caused by parental behavior rather than genetic, temperamental or social variables . . . Such causality is difficult to establish in court so that very few cases are ever brought to trial on the basis of emotional abuse."[8]

A great part of the problem in defining the various areas of emotional maltreatment lies in determining the purpose for that definition. Some experts have suggested that the definition of abuse should be considered separately from that definition which justifies state intervention, and they intend to make helpful, voluntary services available to all who wish to receive them. They believe that the state's right to intervene can only be justifiably exercised if certain "minimum needs" (not specified) are not met. This position is common among people who believe government has no inherent right to intrude into the "sanctity of the family."

While such a position defines abuse as a method of guaranteeing services to those who want them, the Institute of Judicial Administration–American Bar Association standards clearly define abuse for the purpose of indicating when legal intervention is appropriate. The IJA–ABA standards specify that coercive intervention for emotional abuse is warranted only if the child is suffering (or has a serious probability of suffering within days or weeks) serious emotional damage as shown by severe anxiety, depression, withdrawal or untoward aggressive behavior toward himself or others *and* if the child's parents are unwilling to provide treatment for him.[9] This definition does not require proof that parents caused the emotional damage, but it does require expert testimony regarding the condition of the child. With our adversarial system as it is, this situation might mean the judge is subject to a bias toward one expert or another, since reliable, valid criteria for diagnosis and related treatment are lacking. The IJA–ABA definition is a good one, but does not solve the problem of how to consistently and competently measure the emotional maltreatment of children or, more importantly, how to predict and prevent that maltreatment. The various definitions examined all lack conclusiveness. Simply focusing on the effects (harm) is not sufficient; neither is focusing on the intent of the caretaker. A conclusive definition would include both value judgment and behavioral assessment.

What are the differences between emotional abuse and neglect? Is one more harmful than the other? Those of us who work with the children who have suffered from either or both do not consider one form of maltreatment any less destructive than another. Verbal and emotional abuses leave scars that are, if anything, more devastating than those resulting from physical assaults; and childhood rejection haunts people into old age. Today's neglectful parents may have long since recovered from physical injuries suffered as children, but they are still profoundly crippled by emotional injuries inflicted in their early years. Emotional wounds, unlike cuts and bruises, are not outwardly visible. Often they are undetected and remain untreated. Like the untreated physical wound, the untreated emotional wound tends to scar and deform.

Verbal Abuse

The father sat at the barstool with his drinking buddies, his three-year-old daughter amusing herself as best she could while her father shared stories and insults with the patrons. "Wanna see something funny?" he asked the man sitting next to him. "Wanna see me make her cry?" He pointed to his child.

"Winnie, come here." She came obediently. "Winnie, you are a -------" He began calling her a long list of unprintable names, each ending with a "aren't you, Winnie?" The little girl's face crumpled, then she began sobbing as she'd nod in agreement to each obscenity hurled at her.

"I could make her cry without laying a finger on her. Ain't that funny?" her father laughed to his companions. A man at the end of the bar watched the spectacle for a time before interrupting. He was told to mind his own business.

Most experts would agree that the father was abusing his daughter in the form of verbal abuse that uses words as weapons. The messages the child received, her person being equated with obscenities, will probably never be erased. To some degree the girl will always carry that image of herself as worse than worthless. Verbally abused children have no knowledge or internal mechanism to contradict crushing words. If a child is called a stupid, good-for-nothing brat, or worse, she believes that must be true.

Any remarks that destroy a child's self-image are verbally abusive. Such remarks aren't intended to change objectionable behavior, but to destroy self-esteem. The vicious circle of verbal abuse may mean that the hurtful words a parent heard as a child are passed on. The parent's self-esteem is so fragile that trivial events may trigger feelings of insecurity, helplessness and rage. The force of those feelings is so overwhelming that the parent uses strong language in an effort to handle the feelings and release tension.

Emotional Neglect

While Winnie received verbal abuse (negative attention), Kevin experienced little interaction of any kind with his teen-aged mother. She, in turn, had never known warm, positive emotional support and stimulation from her parents. Kevin was fed more or less regularly with a propped bottle, but was left wet and lonely for hours at a time. He was seldom cuddled, and when he was touched he was handled roughly. His mother did not talk to him, look in his eyes, sing or smile at him. He was growing up severely emotionally neglected. For reasons based in the mother's past, she was unwilling or unable to be emotionally present for her child. Nothing harmful was said or done to the child. Nothing much was done, period.

Some of the saddest children I've worked with are such victims of emotional neglect. Often they lack a sense of personhood; they seem to be empty shells of children. Adults who have grown up with a history of emotional neglect appear to lack feelings. One such woman told me, "I don't have anything where my heart should be. I'm just a blank inside." As a child, she saw herself as having no effect on her parents; as an adult she saw herself as a nonperson. Because she grew up being denied the normal experiences which produce feelings of being loved, wanted and competent, she had nothing much inside herself to give to her own children. In its extreme form, emotional neglect of babies and small children leads to "failure-to-thrive," a syndrome by which a child does not develop normally and can die.

Like moral neglect, the American Humane Association has defined emotional neglect as "intangible". The consequences of emotional neglect, however, are often observable in the child's behavior and conduct. "A child may be said to be emotionally neglected when there is failure on the part of parents to provide him with the emotional support necessary for the development of a sound personality. A child may become emotionally neglected when the climate in the home lacks the warmth and security essential for building in the child a sense of being loved and wanted. When attitudes in the home are tense, hostile, unfriendly or threatening; when a child is met with overt or subtle rejection; when by direct or open statement or through less defined but equally meaningful implications, he is made to feel unwanted; when he is made to feel he does not belong; when he is picked upon or is the butt of frequent blame or ridicule; and when, subtly or openly, he is made to feel inferior to others, we have a home climate which inevitably will produce an emotionally neglected child." [10]

As lengthy as this definition is, like others, it raises questions. While we seem to know intuitively that such conditions do produce disturbed children, we have no way of knowing exactly *how* "tense, hostile, unfriendly or threatening," for example, the home attitudes need be to produce emotional damage. Some children's personalities are tender; others labeled "invulnerables" or "resilient children" by professionals seem to withstand profound emotional maltreatment yet somehow emerge more or less mentally and emotionally healthy.

Emotional Abuse

Another area of emotional maltreatment is illustrated by the life of Gary, the stepson of a sheriff's deputy. Determined to "make a man" of the four-year-old, the father devised one scheme after another to frighten the child, then laughed and ridiculed him when he cried or showed fear. The following incident brought the situation to the attention of social services.

After telling Gary repeatedly that a certain clothing closet was filled with "bats that sucked your blood before leaving you to die," the stepfather pushed the terrified boy into the closet and locked it. Hours later, Gary had lost his voice and was bleeding from blood vessels that had broken as a result of his screaming for hours while locked in the closet. The mother brought Gary for medical attention, but she defended her husband by saying he was just trying to keep Gary from "growing into a wimp."

This particular instance of emotional abuse differs from most in that the victim was left with physical symptoms (bleeding and extreme hoarseness). While emotional wounds are internal, they are usually more life-crippling than other forms of abuse, but as pointed out, emotional abuse generally underlies physical abuse and neglect as well. The child who has been emotionally abused often doesn't realize that his person and spirit are being violated. Often the emotional abuser does not realize the destructiveness of his behavior.

As with emotional neglect, no consistent legal criteria exist for the determination of emotional abuse. Many courts refuse to recognize the concept because of the lack of consensus on what it is. Behavioral scientists, social workers and foster parents are frustrated by observing examples of what they strongly believe to be emotional abuse but which courts of law would not recognize as being in the legal domain. A wide gulf exists between what is *known* from a humane point of view, and what can be *proven* in a court of law.

In my experiences with such cases, I have noted a feeling of oppressive heaviness that hangs over family interactions. Verbal manipulation, veiled threats, dishonest communication, references to past offenses, and above all, guilt used as a weapon, are some of the clubs that parents use on children. The assignment of guilt can be so insidious that the child is unaware that it is being used, or so blatant that he wants to run away or commit suicide. In any case, the child is left with feelings of inadequacy, helplessness and sometimes hopelessness. Often, without the intervention of people such as social workers, a suicide will likely occur.

In general, cases of emotional abuse that have been successfully brought to court have had one or more of the following characteristics:

1. an objective measure of the detrimental effect that the emotional abuse has had on the child, including distinct emotional symptoms and/or functional limitations which can with probable cause be linked to parents' treatment;

2. an act or actions considered patently atrocious by community standards; or

3. parents' refusal to seek treatment for a child's demonstrated emotional problems, whether or not they are deemed responsible for the initial problem.

The following illustration might serve as an example of the first characteristic. Andrea was a nine-year-old girl who lived with her father, stepmother and new baby step-brother. She was a bright child who had done well in school until midway through the fourth grade when her father remarried. Then her grades fell rapidly and her appearance deteriorated markedly. When tested by the counselor, various psychological problems were revealed. The child's self-esteem was very low and in a draw-a-picture test, she placed herself significantly outside the family circle. When questioned about it, she indicated she didn't consider herself included in the family since her father's remarriage and the birth of the new baby.

Andrea reported serious verbal abuse by her step-mother, who, among other things, called her a "whore" and a "slut" and predicted she'd end up in the gutter like her birth mother. These findings, combined with other factors (such as excessive school absenteeism, sudden uncharacteristic aggression toward others, and poor hygiene) suggested emotional abuse.

When at her father's request, Andrea was placed in another home for a time, her test scores and appearance improved, her aggressive behavior lessened, and her teachers reported that she was smiling again and interacting normally. After three months, when she was returned to her home, her negative symptoms recurred, this time more intensely.

Because these symptoms were obvious and severe, documented by various objective persons; because a measurable change in function occurred; and because the stepmother's abusive and rejecting behaviors could be documented and related to Andrea's symptoms, this case might have been successfully brought to court in many states.

A recent national advice column reported a situation which could possibly be brought to court for intervention under the second characteristic of maltreatment. A fifth-grade boy who wet the bed at night was frequently made to stand for hours in his front yard wearing only a diaper. In some states such cases, where public humiliation can be documented, have been prosecuted.

In the area where I work, a case involving the parents' refusal to provide treatment for a child's serious emotional problems (the third characteristic) has been a "hot potato." Following a period of severe depression and withdrawal, Justin, an eighth-grade boy, began leaving notes and cryptic poems with friends that suggested he was planning suicide. When one of these notes was brought to the school administrator's attention, Justin was questioned. He admitted he was planning to kill himself. His home life, by his account, was miserably unhappy. His mentally ill mother ruled the household with draconian authority. The boy said he planned to kill himself because he had no other way of escaping from her. (His older sister had shown a pattern of deviance that resulted in her institutionalization for the attempted murder of her baby.)

Because of genuine concern that Justin would carry out his threat, police and, subsequently, a child protection worker were called to school. After interviews with several people, including the parents who insisted the only problem was interfering busybodies, Justin was taken into protective custody. For some time the parents refused any type of treatment for their child and demanded that he be returned immediately to their custody. In a barrage of letters to the newspaper, they stated that their child was merely seeking attention and had manipulated "the system" to avoid his parents' "loving discipline."

Because the school, youth shelter and an independent psychologist all believed Justin was seriously disturbed, the parents' refusal to provide treatment might be considered grounds for emotional neglect, apart from any considerations as to whether their behavior had caused the problem itself.

It appears that for emotional maltreatment to be heard by today's courts, children must be severely injured and/or the parents' behavior must be clearly shown to have caused the injury. Because the adversarial approach can deal with only the most extreme cases, a nonadversarial approach must be developed to encourage parents to change their own behavior.

Garbarino adds that "one last caveat is necessary before plunging into the task of specifying actionable criteria for emotional abuse. This is the necessity to recognize the importance of individual differences—e.g., the impact of the child's 'temperament' in shaping the outcome of parent-child relations. While in the case of physical abuse there are at least some universals—a broken bone is a broken bone is a broken bone—in the matter of emotional abuse there are few, if any. As developmental psychology has grudgingly realized, the impact of any specific parental behavior is to some degree dependent upon the child toward whom it is directed." [11]

•

At the outset of this project, my editor expressed the hope I would be able to succinctly define emotional maltreatment and propose solutions. Mark Twain's comment immediately came to mind. "I was gratified to be able to answer promptly and I did. I said I didn't know."

After months of researching what our foremost child care scientists have written on the subject, that frank answer still applies. We are still a long way from being able to quantify those elusive qualities that lead to individual and family pathology or health. Research is urgently needed in disciplines ranging from socio-biology to law. Until we have an understanding of what minimum and optimum conditions are needed for emotional health, we will continue to largely flounder about, knowing we should do something, but remaining in disagreement over exactly what.

Probably Dr. Charlene Kavanaugh's suggestions for a dual focus for research is most practical. She advocates that (a) systems for evaluation of deviant child behavior within a developmental context be identified, as well as (b) psychiatric disorders in children that can be joined to principles of family diagnosis and family psychology." [12]

The beginnings of that "developmental context" have been around for centuries as folk wisdom. The next chapter explains how temperamental differences referred to by Garbarino affect parent-child relationships and can set the scene for child abuse.

Chapter Four

Are Mothers Always the Problem?

Temperamental Differences in Children

Several women friends of mine and I had dinner together in a pleasant restaurant one evening. Inevitably, conversation turned to our families and children, then to family issues in general.

"It seems mothers are blamed for everything that goes wrong!" one woman commented. The others nodded their heads in agreement. They all felt that society—including professionals who should know better—blames parents, especially mothers, for whatever problems children may develop.

If a baby throws a tantrum over every experience from a new food to the new babysitter, it must be mother's fault. If a potty-trained child suddenly wets the bed, it must be the way mother trained him. If a teenager is sullen and uncommunicative, society implies mother made serious mistakes.

There are probably many reasons for this jaundiced maternal view. Freud blamed mothers for children's neuroses, and Jung agreed. But psychoanalysts aren't the only ones who point to mother as the culprit for whatever may later go wrong in a child's life. People who are aware of attachment disorders described in Chapter Two sometimes overemphasize the effects of temporary absence and blame everything from a child's stuttering to her difficulty in reading on a brief vacation taken by the parents. Many of today's "how-to-parent" books suggest that the author has found a sure-fire way to raise healthy, wealthy and wise children. If the product doesn't turn out quite that way, the implication is clear that mother (or father) messed up or didn't follow the directions.

While the parent-child relationship obviously exerts a profound effect on the child's development, research has established another influential factor, the child's congenital temperament. For over twenty years, two prominent child psychiatrists, Dr. Stella Chess and Dr. Alexander Thomas, have followed the behavioral development of 133 children from early infancy to adulthood. After the babies had left the hospital nursery, the team made regular visits to their homes and schools. They administered various tests to the children and interviewed the parents and the children themselves after they turned sixteen.

A major focus of their study was the identification of congenital temperament and its influence on psychological development. They identified nine typical behavioral characteristics.

In an article detailing the long-term conclusions of their New York Longitudinal Study, Drs. Chess and Thomas define temperament as follows:

"Two children may dress themselves or ride a bicycle with the same dexterity and have the same motives for engaging in these activities. Two adolescents may display similar learning ability and intellectual interests, and their academic goals may coincide . . . Yet these two children (or) adolescents may differ significantly with regard to the quickness with which they move, the ease with which they approach a new physical environment, social situation or task; and the effort required by others to distract them when they are absorbed in an activity. In other words, their abilities and motivations may be similar, yet their temperaments may be different." [1]

For conscientious and caring parents who have wondered, "Why is this child so hard to raise?" the Chess–Alexander findings can be very hopeful. For parents who have done everything they possibly could, yet watched a child grow into a troubled adulthood, the doctors' observations can assuage some guilt.

The married team of Chess–Alexander has established that the temperamental type is well-ingrained at birth; and although it can be molded, it does not change easily. They discovered that despite a newborn's temperament, the most significant factors shaping the child's development is the "goodness of fit" between parent and child. Even temperamentally "difficult" babies did not necessarily develop problems, particularly when parental expectations meshed well with the infant's potential and behavioral style. On the other hand, if parents didn't "fit" well with an infant's special qualities or capabilities, problems often occurred.

Let's briefly examine the nine different congenital temperaments Chess and Thomas describe.

1. Activity level (inherent degree of motor activity present, whether the child is active or passive)

2. Rhythmicity (regularity of biological functions such as hunger, elimination, sleep-wakefulness)

3. Approach or withdrawal (when faced with the need to respond to new situation)

4. Adaptability (length of time and ease with which the child can modify behavior to a new situation)

5. Threshold of responsiveness (how much stimulation is required to evoke a response)

6. Intensity of reaction (energy level used in response)

7. Quality of mood (positive or negative—for example, pleasant or joyful, as contrasted with irritable or sad)

8. Distractibility (ease with which ongoing behavior is changed by extraneous behavior)

9. Attention span and persistence (two related categories. Attention span concerns the length of time a child pursues a particular activity; persistence refers to continuing in that activity in the face of obstacles)[2]

Chess and Thomas assigned to these nine characteristics numerical values that can be used to evaluate newborns. From this information, they determined three constellations of temperament. "Easy" babies were those who would be easy to care for and easy to raise. They had regular schedules, dealt positively with change and had only mild mood swings. They comprised about 40% of the children studied.

"Difficult" babies, those that were hard to relate to and later hard to raise, were biologically irregular, slow to change their behavior and showed strong negative behavior. They comprised about 10% of the study group. For optimal development, they required more from their mothers than would "easy" babies. The other 50% of the babies fell somewhere between "easy" and "difficult."

The traits as described by Chess and Thomas profoundly affect the way a child is treated. For example, a child who is highly emotional in a negative way, who is withdrawn, or who can't stick to any task for any length of time, is less likely to be asked to spend the day at a friend's house as compared with a child who is "easy," and charming. We can see how, within a short time, a child's congenital temperament begins to affect not only parents, but the larger social environment.

Following the initial temperament classification, Chess and Thomas observed the ways children progressed with various types of mothering. They found, not surprisingly, that nurturing mothers who had "easy" babies did very well. Most of these children experienced uneventful, happy childhoods. The children who had "difficult" temperaments tended to have more adjustment and behavioral problems throughout their lives, especially when born to nonnurturing women.

The couple found examples of "mismatched" children where parents and children had endured tumultuous infancies and toddlerhoods which were characterized by one tantrum or upset after another. To their gratification, they discovered that by early adolescence some children had settled down to being "normal." This finding indicates that we give up on children too early. One "difficult" little girl, hypersensitive and explosive, was labeled a "rotten kid" by her parents. They were critical and rigid with her, and she responded with behavioral problems. When as a fifth-grader, she showed signs of musical talent and received plenty of praise from teachers, her self-esteem increased and the behavior problems decreased. Discovering her "gift" in early adolescence made a tremendous difference in her life.

A friend of mine, the mother of a delightful little boy, expressed consternation almost right after the birth of her second son some years ago. Although Janet's pregnancy and delivery were normal and she had been extremely careful about her health habits during pregnancy, her second baby seemed withdrawn and irritable from the first time she held him.

"I wondered what was wrong with me that he reacted the way he did. This was a baby we wanted and planned, born with no known physical problems. Yet I knew something was wrong."

As Mark grew from infancy to toddlerhood, so did his parents' concern. Pediatricians told them to just "relax" and suggested colic, overly high parental expectations, and other causes for their baby's passivity and solemn, unresponsive manner.

Scientists haven't yet discovered why newborns should be despondent or repelled by their new surroundings, and they are concentrating on seeking possible genetic and environmental factors. Babies such as Mark are born not only to mentally ill or substance-abusing mothers, but to normal, healthy women such as Janet.

Her first reaction to her withdrawn baby was to flood him with stimulation in an attempt to win some responsiveness. He responded all right—by crying and further withdrawing. This reaction created even more guilt and frustration for the parents. It would have been easy just to meet Mark's physical needs at that point and forget about attachment.

"Those were days I just wanted to walk away," Mark's mother remembers. "Every time I looked at him I felt like a failure."

Fortunately, the couple learned later from a therapeutic nursery team that babies born with their child's temperament are easily overstimulated. What appeared to be withdrawal was actually an attempt by the overly sensitive child to retreat from too much confusion. When the parents provided a quiet, low-key atmosphere, Mark's symptoms began showing improvement.

Some—not enough—programs across the country have been established to help parents of children classified as "difficult" right after birth. The goal of these programs includes giving parents a perspective on how they and their babies react to each other (often by means of videotapes of interactions). Probably the most important reason for such programs is to prevent the baby's mystifying behavior from escalating into a problem that affects the whole family.

The importance of temperament has been recognized by other child experts including Dr. T. Berry Brazelton, whose books advise parents that children who have differing temperaments require different parental management. He documented adjustments made by parents whose babies are not cuddly or loveable at birth, and devised the Brazelton Neonatal Behavioral Assessment Scale (usually referred to as "the Brazelton"). This test measures 26 behavioral and reflex activities of the newborn infant. It is commonly used to identify babies whose behavior may be reducing their chances of getting off to a good start with their parents.

He describes the innate differences in the babies he studied. "At birth we see infants who overreact to every noise or stimulus—starting visibly, crying out, changing color, spitting up, and having a bowel movement—all as part of a reaction to a single stimulus. Other infants will react to the same stimulus by lying quietly in their cribs, eyes widening, faces alerting, color paling and bodily activity reducing to a minimum, seeming to conserve all energy in order to pay attention to the stimulus. They are both normal reactions, at different ends of a spectrum . . . A challenging environment will reinforce certain physiological patterns as the infant tries to handle the stress. The mechanisms that one infant uses will differ markedly from those that another may use. For instance, one infant may resort to crying— insistently and for long periods—as a way of shutting out the tension of an overwrought mother. Another may begin to withdraw into more and more sleep. Both reactions are ways of coping with stress that might otherwise overload the baby's system and they may become the pattern on which a particular child falls back whenever under stress." [3]

Dr. Brazelton, like Drs. Chess and Thomas, cautions that while parents cannot change these individual differences, they do have control over their own reactions to these differences.

How can parents of a "difficult" child work toward the "good fit" that makes for a healthy attachment? How can parents reach out to a baby who cries inconsolably when picked up? What can a mother do to help her baby come to accept her and stop blaming herself for her child's negative response?

Dr. Brazelton writes, "Mothers tell me they *know* it's their fault; this very feeling of guilt and inadequacy can build up to a feeling of helplessness and even anger toward the baby . . . these feelings create anxiety and press a parent to redouble her efforts to reach the baby. In turn, the efforts overload the baby even more and she turns off even more dramatically. The stage can be set for feelings of failure on both their parts . . ."

His nursery research showed that babies such as these were hypersensitive, and their periods of availability for responsiveness were very short and unpredictable. They tended to eat greedily, then spit up everything. They had touchy gastrointestinal tracts, often showing signs of colic and diarrhea. These babies often slept, ate and cried (not much else) for at least the first three months.

What finally proved effective with these unrewarding infants was the same approach that worked for Mark's mother. Babies could be touched or held or looked at or talked to, for example, but not all at the same time. The rhythm, quality and quantity of the stimulation was turned way down.

When this gentle, low-key approach was used, the babies began to decrease their avoidance behavior.

Confining or swaddling in blankets is often helpful to hypersensitive babies, as is the use of a pacifier or thumb for sucking. Feeding and talking to difficult babies in dimly lit rooms and attempting to keep parental tension at a minimum have all improved the disposition of hypersensitive babies.

Parents can encourage a secure attachment with their babies by listening and watching carefully for the cues they provide. If parents can learn early with "difficult" babies and are willing to be adaptable, that is to mold their expectations and schedules to fit those of the child, problems can be avoided. If these parents are expecting too much of their child, perhaps they could use some emotional feeding of their own. It's hard for a parent to be patient and gentle with children when she feels angry, frustrated or bad about herself.

Perhaps the most encouraging word for mothers tired of being blamed for everything or worried about doing wrong by their children comes from Dr. Brazelton, who says "Do what makes you and your baby feel the best and gives you the nicest time together."

That simple prescription goes a long way toward prevention of child abuse.

Chapter Five

"Be What I Need You to Be"

Aspects of Emotional Maltreatment

In any treatment of child abuse, a tendency exists to concentrate on the most bizarre and horrendous examples of physical maltreatment. As a social worker who has been involved with incidents that were sickening in their severity, it would be easy to describe some gruesome abuses, ones that create revulsion and rage on the part of readers. This approach, though common, is not helpful. At the same time, an examination of the types of emotional maltreatment and conditions under which they are likely to occur may aid in solutions for the problem.

Hostility–Verbal Abuse

The following description of a mother's hostility was given me by a woman who is today trying to improve relationships within her own family.

"'Why was she always so angry at me?' I wondered as a child. I never wanted to look at her, because I saw only hate or contempt in her eyes. I got out of the habit of looking at people's faces when I was young. I know it bothers people today that I can't look at them, but I'm afraid I'll see that same hatred and contempt from my childhood.

"I remember an incident when I was nine. I had two younger sisters, and had to spend a lot of time taking care of them and doing housework. I'd worked all that Saturday, and finally went to my room to read—the only pleasure I had. It was my escape from a lonely, painful world, and I'd looked forward all day to getting away from reality. But I didn't feel good. I was dizzy and left with a heaviness that I just wanted to drop onto my bed.

"I had just entered the room I shared with my sisters when I heard my mother angrily calling me. I wanted to pretend I couldn't hear her and just crawl beneath the covers. But she was coming down the hall, shrieking at me to get to the living room. 'You call that dusting?' she jeered. 'You didn't do the bookshelves. Get out there and do the job right.'

" 'I don't feel good,' I said, hoping she'd relent.

" 'I don't feel so good either when I see what a good-for-nothing job you do. Get up. Now.'

"While I went back to redo the dusting, my mother waxed the hallway. She had a cleanliness fetish, and most of her waking hours were devoted to scrubbing, scouring and waxing. There was never time for people, or for talking, just cleaning. Dirt was her mortal enemy, and she went after it with a religious fervor.

"After I had redusted, I returned to my room. Maybe because my head was spinning I didn't notice the wax in the hallway wasn't completely dry. It was only a minute after I'd sunk into the bed before my mother burst into the room, her eyes glinting with rage. 'You stupid girl, you walked on the wet floor. You're stupid, stupid, stupid. You don't care about me, do you? You don't care that I work my fingers to the bone. Nobody cares!'

"The tirade went on for so long that the old words seemed to hang in the air as new ones spewed out of her mouth. I tried to shut them out by watching insects buzz around the light fixture over my bed. I remember wishing I was a bug so I could just fly away from her.

"She slapped me hard across the face before storming out of my room. Sometime during the night my father woke me up and told me to take some aspirin. He looked in my eyes as I tried to raise my head off the pillow. 'She doesn't mean it,' he said. That's the only time I can remember him referring to the way my mother treated me.

"But I knew she did mean it. She never missed an opportunity to tell me how miserably I treated her, how her life was nothing but a sacrifice for her family, and how no one appreciated everything she did for us. I was lonely and confused those years. No matter how hard I tried to please her, she would shrug and tell me how I could have done it better. Nothing I did was quite good enough. I became terribly nervous and anxious to please her, yet more than anything I just wanted to escape her critical attention. Looking back at pictures of myself taken as a young teenager, I see a wax statue, expressionless and detached.

"My mother is widowed now and lives in a distant city. She comes to see me about once a year. Although some of the hostility is there, she hides it behind a tight, artificial smile. She doesn't scream at me anymore, but she still makes me feel guilty for not keeping a house that meets her impossible standards. With her humorless smile, she suggests to me ways I might do things better.

"I know now she's a terribly unhappy woman who I wish had been helped years ago. She's an intelligent, strong woman, but her desire to control and her hostility have crippled me. I'm in my late thirties, so I still have time to forgive her and get my life straightened out."

Many parents feeling the kind of hostility described above punish their children with disparagement, severe criticism, threat, ridicule and a barrage of negative comments. Often "respectable" parents who wouldn't dream of physically abusing their children or "who don't want the neighbors to know" inflict emotional abuse far more destructive in its effects.

Unrealistic Expectations

One of the saddest children I've dealt with was Teddy, the son of a professional couple who had put off starting their family until both parental careers were firmly established. Teddy was almost instantly a disappointment to his parents.

Instead of his mother's good looks, he inherited his father's craggy-featured face. Instead of a docile nature that would "fit well" with those of his parents, he had a temperament that could be described as somewhat "difficult." When placed in an expensive day care center at the age of three months, he began to suffer from one bout after another of respiratory problems. His parents rather grudgingly took turns staying home with him, but according to day care workers, he would be returned prematurely, clinging and fretful, so that his parents could return to work.

At the age of four, Teddy was presented with a computer, but he disappointed his parents by showing little interest in it. From what his mother says, about that time the parents began using guilt and criticism on their son. "He can just stay in his room," she told me. "He doesn't care about everything we've given him, or how hard we work for him. He just sits and looks at me with those sad eyes.

"And messy! I can't believe he doesn't make messes just to get to me! I think sometimes he wants to see me go crazy. He knows I don't allow snacking, yet he took a box of crackers to his room and crawled under his bed to eat them. You should have seen the crumbs. I had to get down on my hands and knees to vacuum and he wasn't the least bit sorry."

Her voice sharpened and grew angrier. "I'm not going to put up with his messiness. I just won't. He's got to learn to be neat."

I asked her what she could do to help him be neater and she looked at the floor. "Yesterday he dribbled milk when he was eating cereal. I know he did it on purpose; he looked up at me right after he did it. I got so angry I took his bowl and put it on the floor. I told him to get down on his hands and knees and eat like an animal, because that's what he is. An *animal.* And I'm going to treat him like one until he decides to act like a human being.

"His father will get on me about this, though. He gets angry at *me* when Teddy acts like that. Even though he gets angry himself, he says to me, 'Let up on him, he's only four.' And then I see that look in Teddy's eyes like, 'See, he's on my side. So I *can* drive you crazy.'"

Teddy's mother is attributing intentionality and negative disposition to her small son. Her unrealistic expectations for Teddy are not only damaging his self esteem, but driving a deep wedge into her marriage. In fact it's likely that the hatefulness she shows her son is misplaced anger at her husband. This anger, combined with a "poor fit" in the Chess-Thomas terminology, leads to a strong likelihood of problems unless the family receives help.

Dorothy Corkille Briggs, author of *Your Child's Self-Esteem,* emphasizes the abusiveness of parents who force a child to meet unrealistic expectations. "While he buckles under to fit preconceived expectations that disregard his essential nature, his self-respect is maimed. Being true to himself means maintaining the integrity of his uniqueness; it is the taproot for his stability. Submitting to expectations that run contrary to his nature always causes impairment. Rigid, unrealistic expectations fairly shriek, 'Be as I need you to be. Don't be you!'"[1]

Emotional Neglect

A young teacher I know socially called recently about a child in her classroom. She was disturbed about Tim, a little boy whom she considered emotionally neglected. Her principal, seeing no bruises, was reluctant to "rock the boat." She was uncertain about what to do, but was convinced the child needed someone to come to his aid.

I asked her to explain why she felt that way, and she said the child had been unusually quiet in her classroom one morning. When asked if he was feeling all right, he'd nodded 'yes'. Later in the morning, however, he fainted and was brought to the hospital where it was discovered he had a ruptured appendix.

"The thing is," she explained, "from what he'd told me I knew that he was simply not able to ask for any kind of help. The pain he suffered before he was hospitalized must have been awful. But he was so used to being ignored at home that he didn't tell me how sick he was.

"The grandmother of the boy had called earlier to 'explain' about Tim. Apparently she is the only one in the family who cares about him. When Tim was in the hospital, according to the nurse, his parents came to see him once—and then because they'd been asked to come by a nurse. They are just 'not there' for him. Is there anything I can do?"

Tim has a teacher and a grandmother who show concern and affection for him. Because of them, he is more fortunate than many neglected children. He has a better chance than most of the children studied by Dr. Byron Egeland and his associates at the University of Minnesota. They described the psychologically unavailable parents (mothers in their study) as being "unresponsive to their children, and in many cases, passively rejecting of them. These mothers appeared detached and uninvolved with their children, interacting with them only when it was necessary. In general, the mothers were withdrawn, displayed flat affect and seemed depressed. There was no indication that these mothers derived any pleasure from their relationship with their children."[2] The babies that Dr. Egeland studied grew up without warmth. They represent sad commentaries on the effects of unresponsive parents. They are anxious and insecure, delayed in development and unable to handle frustration. Typically, some are overly aggressive, and others are withdrawn and silent.

Nonorganic Failure-to-Thrive

One of the most dramatic forms taken by emotional maltreatment is a syndrome known as failure-to-thrive. This pattern of psychological unavailability frequently begins when a child is hospitalized or for other reasons is psychologically absent from her parents.

For many reasons, very young failure-to-thrive babies may not demand much in the way of parental attention. As they grow older, they demand less and less because that is what they've learned to expect.

A diagnosis of nonorganic failure-to-thrive (FTT) is made when a child under three years of age fails to grow because of inadequate caloric intake with no organic cause. In other words, a pervasive emotional deprivation causes these babies to listlessly shrivel up. Even if fed what would seem to be enough calories for a normal baby, these FTT infants do not grow and develop normally. Lack of nurturing, stimulation and attachment prevent the child from thriving. Without intervention, such victims of emotional neglect and abuse do die.

Dr. Clare Haynes and her associates have theorized that "psychological conflicts or social stresses are presumed to have interfered with the mother's ability to provide adequate care for the child. The precise mechanism through which these unresolved conflicts or stresses influence the relationship in a way which leads to the child's growth failure is not well understood."[3]

Among other factors, her research compared mother-child interactions in 25 thriving and 50 FTT babies. Their study found that in contrast to the thriving mothers, none of the FTT mothers had good memories of their own childhoods.

"Mothers in the 'benign neglect' group were inappropriately dependent on their babies to guide their caregiving actions. They lacked an understanding of their babies' nutritional needs and seemed to expect that their babies know their own needs . . . These mothers would brag about what 'good' babies they had because they made so few demands. They might, for example, not be at all upset if their babies slept throughout the night even if told the crucial importance of night feedings and despite the mothers themselves perceiving the babies as 'getting lighter.' "

The videotaped feedings of this group showed mothers who appeared to be relieved when babies went to sleep, whether or not their caloric intake had been adequate. They would generally make no effort to keep them alert to finish feeding. As explained in Chapter Two, without nurturing behavior from the mother, the rewarding smiles and eye contact from the infant diminishes, and gradually the baby withdraws even further. Dr. Haynes and her associates found the same unhappy situation.

"In the absence of appropriate stimulation and guidance from their mothers, the babies became less competent and rewarding to their mothers who correspondingly further neglected them and left them alone."[4]

A second identified group of mothers of FTT infants was labeled as 'incoordinated.' They had the capacity to perform appropriate actions in feeding and play; however, they did not appropriately match their actions to their babies' cues. These mothers would perhaps feed by the clock regardless of other circumstances, such as how inadequate the previous feeding had been. If the babies showed signs of feeding distress, such as choking or coughing, they did not take what seemed common-sense actions, such as stopping the feeding. Often they would distract their babies with loud noises, whistles, hair-tugging or other bids for attention, then not resume feedings. The babies seemed to know their mothers were not attuned to their needs and gave up easily.

The third pattern of FTT mothers was 'overtly hostile.' Not only did they fail to recognize their babies' cues for feeding, burping and proper holding, but they also showed outright hostile behavior toward them. For example, when unknowingly observed, these mothers withheld food from their babies who were already in a state of near-starvation. They ate the food themselves and reported that the child had eaten it. In one case, a mother poured milk into the child's diaper in an attempt to deceive the nurse. Their behaviors included making scary faces, spitting or blowing in their children's faces, making frightening noises with spoons, and so on. In response to their mothers' actions, the babies turned away, appeared confused or "shut down".

In both the hostile and incoordinated groups, the mothers failed to respond to the babies' clear cues of disinterest, displeasure, or even pain;

instead, they continued their tickling, growling, aggressive attacks, or whatever was causing discomfort in the child. In fact, in many cases the babies' cues seemed to only intensify the mothers' improper actions.

Long-term follow-up of the mothers and babies revealed 78% of FTT babies had retarded physical growth and about 60% had significant developmental delays. Of the 44 families for which information was available, two children had died, five had been reported for physical abuse, and ten children were no longer in the care of their parents. (The causes of the two deaths were listed as Sudden Infant Death Syndrome in a baby described as severely malnourished, and accidental hanging in the child's crib.)

The conclusions drawn from this and similar important studies of the various aspects taken by maltreatment are many. Most significantly, the researchers discovered when early diagnosis and intervention is made (within six months of age) babies are more likely to catch up to normal birth weight and development. They also found that the mother's own experience of being nurtured is profoundly related to the adequacy of nurturance in her own children.

Parental Gratification

Parental gratification as a form of emotional maltreatment occurs when the parents' behavior toward the child is a result of desperate attempts to force the child to act in such a way to allow the parents to feel successful. The child is appreciated only when pleasing the parents. Many knowledge-able people with whom I visited before writing this book believe it to be the most pervasive yet subtle form of emotional abuse. The child maltreated in such a way is not seen or valued as a person with rights, feelings or interests of her own, but is merely an extension of the parent. When the child is perfectly obedient, stays out of the way or takes care of the parent, she is valued. But only then.

David Elkind's *The Hurried Child* and Marie Winn's *Children Without Childhood* [5,6] describe children in our society who exist to meet parental needs. Dr. Elkind details the situation of ten-year-old Janet. She has many responsibilities that go far beyond taking care of her clothing and her room. Among them are getting herself and her young sister off to school on time (her mother leaves earlier for work). Every afternoon Janet's duties include making dinner, babysitting, and serving as her mother's "confidante" about her work and social life when she finally gets home in the evening.

Dr. Elkind says that what is harmful about this case is not the work itself, but the overwhelming responsibility. "Janet feels responsible for her little sister, for her mother, for the house. This is really what distinguishes the hard-working children of today from the immigrant children of previous generations. In the newly-arrived families there was usually a mother and father so that the children did not have parental responsibilities. But in the one-parent home of today, children often have to assume parental responsibilities, forcing them to call too often on adaptation energy reserves."

The phenomenon of the child caring for parents physically and emotionally is quite common. Reversal of roles—the child being the emotional support of the parent—is seen with increasing frequency by social workers and therapists. These children who are forced into meeting their parents' needs seem to have had their childhoods stolen from them.

Becky is the thirteen-year-old daughter of a woman who suffers from a degenerative nerve disease. Although she is in a state of remission, the mother is often extremely irritable and depressed. Since she was ten, Becky has been responsible for the housekeeping and cooking chores. She comes home immediately after school to care for her younger brother and perform her chores. While she has uncomplainingly done these things during her mother's acute state of illness, she resents the fact that the same behavior is expected now that her mother is physically able to do many of the chores. She is not permitted to spend any time with her friends at a time in her life when friendships are crucial to normal development.

When she has done all the work and finished her schoolwork, she occasionally asks for permission to spend some time with friends. By her mother's admission, these are "good kids". But the reaction of Becky's mother to her request is predictable. She calls her daughter "uncaring" and "irresponsible" and begins cataloguing every slight she feels Becky has committed against her.

Unfortunately, Becky has begun to believe there is something wrong with herself for wanting to be with friends when she has a sick mother. She wonders if she is really the uncaring monster her mother makes her out to be. She doubts her worth as a person. The mother does not recognize that by using her daughter solely for her own gratification she is severely inhibiting Becky's social growth and self-esteem.

Therapists explain that the dynamics of parental gratification are complex. Instead of the child being "mothered", a symbiotic process in which a mature, capable person cares for a helpless, dependent, immature person, the child is required to bring meaning and comfort to the parent, regardless of the cost to that child. Sometimes this type of abuse involves a "double-bind." The abusive parent who needs a scapegoat for the expression of personal impulses or wishes will encourage certain behavior in the child who is then punished or ridiculed, resulting in a schizophrenic world for the child. To please the parent, she must play out the "misbehavior" and alternately receive punishment and/or approval.

This double-bind situation often involves messages given at different levels. One may be verbal, the other non-verbal. Constraints are placed on the child which keep her from commenting on the contradiction. The child cannot escape either from the situation or its damaging consequences.

In my experience, this double-bind dynamic often becomes obvious during the onset of the child's adolescence, and is often related to sexual problems between parents or the sexual abuse of a child. Until adolescence, the use of contradictory messages can be used to maintain family equilibrium. As the child enters the teenage years and begins showing some independence (evidence of a changing role within the family), the parents may intensify the double-binding behavior. This is done in a desperate attempt to keep the child in a no-win situation and the family in some sort of balance, unhealthy though it may be. The child has two possible responses to the chronic double-bind: withdrawal or lashing out in rage at the unfairness of it all.

GARBARINO'S FOUR PRINCIPLES OF COMPETENCE

Dr. James Garbarino's research uses the development of competence as a fulcrum with which to move the problem of emotional abuse. "It permits us to evaluate parental behavior (or parent-child relations, or teacher-student relations) in light of a developmental criterion, namely, the contribution to the development of comptetence . . . the key to understanding emotional abuse. If we start with this conception of competency as the 'currency' of development, we can proceed toward an understanding of emotional abuse."[7]

He suggests four principles of emotional abuse that present a "clear and present danger" to the child's developing competence. The first applies to infancy.

"Principle One: Punishment of positive . . . behaviors such as smiling,
   mobility, exploration, vocalization and manipulation of objects
   is emotional abuse."

Dr. Justin Call has written about "games babies play," one of which is the cough game. He describes it as one of the first forms of positive communication with the baby. "For the infant it is one of the first signs of regularity and of his own power to control his world."[8]

The cough game goes something like this: After the baby of perhaps two months happens to cough, the mother playfully imitates him. At first, he notices only the mother's smile and cough, but before long he coughs in return, starting an exchange of smiles and coughs that eventually leaves them both laughing. Dr. Call writes that when the baby is a little older, he initiates the cough-smile when the mother is not expecting it. She is delighted with her baby for his cleverness and the game is resumed. Obviously, this game is of limited interest to the developing child as he goes on to more complex activities. Before losing interest, however, the baby has learned something vastly more important than the game itself—the imitation of oral sounds, necessary if he is to learn to speak.

From his research, Dr. Call has concluded that the play characteristic for each age gives us clues to the child's level of functioning and to his response to others. To learn to play, an infant requires familiarity with the environment and consistent care. Another requirement is satisfaction of physiological needs. Obviously, a baby who is hungry or tired cannot concentrate on playing games. A baby who is punished for trying to play, for smiling, vocalizing and exploring, is being abused. He is learning the world is not responsive or helpful. He is learning his actions have no effect on the world around him. Garbarino believes to ignore or punish behaviors such as smiling, mobility and manipulation is a "clear and present danger to the child's development of competence."

"Principle Two: Discouraging caregiver-infant bonding
is emotional abuse."

Beginning in the early 1970s, two Cleveland pediatricians, Drs. Marshall
Klaus and John Kennell, began a series of observations to understand the
process of attachment that begins between a mother and her newborn child.
These doctors had discovered that despite their best efforts to save
premature babies, far too many of them ended up back in the hospital for
treatment of injuries inflicted by their parents. Drs. Klaus and Kennell
began to wonder if the separation of mother and baby as hospital practice
required contributed to whatever problem was causing the high incidence of
child abuse. What *wasn't* happening between these mothers and preemie
babies that seemed to usually happen with mothers and full-term babies?

They convinced a hospital to change normal routine for fourteen months.
These mothers were given their naked babies to lie next to them for an hour
after delivery and for several hours each day thereafter. (A special heat
panel kept babies and mothers from getting chilled.) A companion group of
fourteen mothers and babies was treated in the routine way with a brief
contact or glance at birth, then twenty-minute feedings every three or four
hours.

One month later, Drs. Klaus and Kennell measured reactions of the
mothers who had enjoyed extended contact with their babies to those of the
control group. They found that the extended contact mothers more often
held their babies face-to-face, held them more frequently, and were more
reluctant to return them to the nurses. The doctors were surprised that *every
one* of these mothers showed that behavior, as though a powerful maternal
instinct had been touched in them.

The two sets of mothers and babies were again compared one month
later. Again, the extended contact mothers showed greater attention to their
babies, standing nearer them at the examining table, soothing them if they
cried. They had more eye contact and fondled them more.

A year later a third comparison was done. Results were similar to earlier
observations. When the babies were two years old, the fourth comparison
was made. This time significant differences were reported in the way
mothers talked to their children. Extended contact mothers asked more
questions, used more adjectives and gave fewer commands than other
mothers.

Many scientists believe the research from this study indicates that a "maternal-sensitive" time exists in the first few hours after birth. It is presumably during this time that the mother is most likely to "fall in love" with her infant. Evidently, these feelings spring from the behavior of acting in a loving way—touching, gazing, embracing. Although the evidence is not conclusive, it indicates that mothers who are encouraged to hold their babies immediately after birth, and for extended periods during the next few days, are likely to form strong, enduring attachments. In addition, mothers who have had these experiences appear more capable and nurturing when their babies grow older.

By no means do all experts agree on the validity of Klaus' and Kennell's findings. In fact, the second edition of *Maternal-Infant Bonding,* renamed *Parent-Infant Bonding,* revised what many researchers felt to be an extreme position. Although the pediatricians continued to believe that bonding during the first hours after birth is very important, they suggested several ways that such attachment could occur later, if for some reason mother and child did not share that after-birth experience.

Their second edition states that "obviously, in spite of the lack of early contact experienced by parents in hospital births in the past twenty to thirty years, almost all of these parents became bonded to their babies. The human is highly adaptable and there are many fail-safe routes to attachment."[9]

Adoptive parents and those who for other reasons could not enjoy extended contact after birth with their babies can be reassured by these words. No reputable researcher today feels that early bonding solves all potential parent-child problems. Rather, the love that comes from early contact may set the pattern for the overall way parents relate to their children. This can relate to any conscientious, caring parent.

In summary, Klaus' and Kennell's findings, as well as attachment research already described, lead child care professionals to believe that discouragement of attachment is emotional abuse, whether the action is performed by the mother herself or by another person or institution. From attachment research, a commonly accepted view has developed that unless parents have a basic love-bond relationship with their child, everything else (discipline, peer relationships, school performance) is on a faulty foundation and problems will likely result.

"Principle Three: Punishment of self-esteem is emotional abuse."

Garbarino believes that discouraging self-esteem is to attack a fundamental component of competent development.

Dr. Stanley Coopersmith's research explains why assaults on a child's self-esteem are so abusive. He discovered that parents of children who had high self-esteem showed affection and concern on an everyday basis. Parents of low self-esteem children tended to give criticism instead of affection. Another important difference he noted was that children who had high self-esteem had been raised in less permissive homes than children with low self-esteem. In the high self-esteem homes, rules were fair and consistently enforced. Coopersmith found, on the other hand, that parents of children with low self-esteem swung between harsh and permissive treatment. Children could sometimes "get away with murder" for certain behaviors that at other times would earn them brutal punishment.[10]

One reason for inconsistent treatment that begets low self-esteem is the fact that children are used by parents to meet their own expectations. If a parent's expectations and wishes are constantly changing, the child doesn't know where she stands. Uncertainty does not breed confidence or competence.

Even parents who may love their children dearly do and say things that tear at the child's self-esteem. Parental insensitivity with regard to children's physical attractiveness and intelligence, in particular, can crush their feelings in a manner that stays with them throughout their lives. For some adults, however, outbursts of scolding, humiliating or putting down are the rule, not the exception.

A friend of mine, one often described as "beautiful", tells me that despite others' opinions, she has problems thinking of herself as anything but plain, or even ugly. She remembers vividly an incident from her childhood. Little Jane, wiping dishes as her mother and aunt drank their tea, was mortified to hear them talking about her. "It's a shame she's so . . . plain," Jane's mother lamented. "Maybe she'll look better when she's older," the aunt comforted.

That kind of disrespect for a child's feelings wounds self-esteem in a way that scars for life. Just a few days ago a colleague reported that he had told the child of an office typist how pretty she looked.

"Don't tell her that; she's not pretty," snapped the mother in front of her child. The next day the mother cornered my colleague. "I wish you wouldn't have said that to my daughter. I won't be able to handle her. She's really going to think she's something special now."

Instead of trying to make her child feel loved and special—which she is—this mother appears to punish any frail indication of self-esteem that might appear in her daughter. According to Garbarino, this would be classified as emotional abuse.

"**Principle Four:** Punishing interpersonal skills necessary for adequate
   performance in non-familiar contexts such as schools, peer
   groups, etc. is emotional abuse."

Someone has said we have no way of knowing if we are tall or short, fat or thin except in relationship with others. Most of what we need for our daily living is learned as we rub elbows with each other. If interpersonal skills have been punished in such a way that our competency is threatened, the individual may remain a "prisoner of childhood."

If normal attachment to parents has taken place, the task of children from the ages of six to twelve is to begin the process of growing away from the family. At this age, the child begins to define herself from reflections coming to her from outside the family: her friends, teachers, and others in the world.

Some parents unconsciously keep the child from preparing for that outside world by inhibiting interpersonal skills. They make the child feel guilty for trying to cut or extend the apron strings, discourage her from getting involved in anything in which she might fail; or they interfere and control relationships to an extent that the child doesn't learn interpersonal skills.

An area of emotional maltreatment many "loving parents" fall into is that of overprotection. While the parent of a generation or two ago worried about children getting lost in cornfields or being beaten up by the neighborhood bully, today's parents have nightmares of pedophiles lurking near shopping malls and school yards, adolescents who "turn on" younger children to drugs, and other horrors generally not imagined a few years back. What's a parent to do in such a dangerous world? Guard and protect, of course.

Parents' desires to shield children from dangers, real and imagined, can interfere with their children's emotional growth and development of competence. Some risks must be tolerated, and chances must be taken if a child is to grow up to be independent of her parents. Well-meaning adults sometimes do damage by suggesting that the child cannot possibly succeed, be safe, or so on, without the parents hovering nearby. Sometimes they demand such blind obedience to their authority that the child doesn't learn how to think.

This kind of "smother love" leads to a double-bind for the child. The parent (usually the mother) appears to give herself totally to the child. When the child, if normal in his feelings begins to chafe under these bonds, the mother turns on him, wielding guilt as a club. "I've done everything for you, expected nothing in return, and now you don't appreciate me. Why don't you love me?"

A preadolescent who has come from such overprotection will find it hard to take any risks or manage difficult situations. Since mother (or dad) has made all decisions, bad consequences have been avoided, as well as self-discipline. If changes aren't made, when this child leaves home in late adolescence, he will be ill-prepared for sudden freedom and responsibility.

The types of emotional maltreatment outlined here vary in destructiveness. Depending on duration, severity, congenital temperament and a host of other factors, differing consequences can be expected. In all cases, significant maltreatment does not result from isolated incidents, which most adults can relate to having committed, but rather from a pattern of wounding and withholding.

Chapter Six

Modern Methods of Maltreatment

Pushing Children as a Form of Abuse and Neglect

When I began working on this book, one of my original intentions was to describe the cruel forms taken by emotional maltreatment: psychological abandonment, humiliation, destruction of self-esteem and so on, all types of abuse and neglect to which children have been subjected throughout the ages. But during the writing, several incidents brought to my attention the fact that parents living in the late twentieth century have the opportunity of abusing or neglecting their children in ways that were unlikely for their grandparents.

I recall an incident that began with a telephone call from a friend one Saturday afternoon. "I hope you're not busy," she began. "I need to talk. I need some advice."

Her daughter, Heidi, a child of eight, had spent the previous night at a slumber party. My friend knew the parents who had called and invited Heidi a few days earlier. She and her husband had no reservations about their daughter spending the night with the Hendersons.

But when Heidi returned home at noon on Saturday, she acted strangely. "She gave me a guilty, sort of furtive look, then ran up to her room. That just isn't like her. I wondered right away what was going on.

"Later, I asked her how the slumber party had gone and she just said, 'Okay,' and evasively changed the subject. It wasn't until the middle of the afternoon that she came up to me and gave me a shy hug."

"What's bothering you?" Heidi's mother had asked.

"Last night at the slumber party we watched this TV show . . ." she hesitated, then stopped. Her mother encouraged her to go on.

After the parents had gone to their room for the night, Heidi said, the girls had gone back into the living room and turned the TV to an "adult" cable channel. They had never seen anything like what appeared on the screen. A man and three women, all naked, were crawling over each other, women kissing each other in unimaginable places, all of them moaning and screaming.

"Mom," Heidi asked, "why were they doing those things?"

Heidi was confused and repulsed, and her mother angry. "I called the girl's mother," she told me, "and she didn't seem to care. I couldn't believe her attitude. She said, 'I'm sorry, we didn't know what the girls were watching.' That was the end of it as far as she was concerned. She didn't seem the least bit disturbed that her eight-year-old was learning about perverted sexuality when she wasn't old enough to understand healthy adult sex. Her mother didn't seem to feel any obligation whatever to shield her daughter from the sordidness of life."

During the following week, I happened to turn on the television one night. Since we don't receive "adult" channels, our family is spared the explicitness of scenes like those Heidi watched. But the program I saw that night was nearly as unsettling to me because of its network respectability.

It was one of those "talent search" shows with all the contestants aged ten and under. These prepubescent children were vying for a modeling award, and as I watched them slither and swivel through their routines with their proud parents beaming in the audience, I didn't know whether to laugh or throw up.

The children vamped and postured in attempts at provocative poses, the effects of false eyelashes and buckets of eye shadow jarring on their sweet faces. Necklines plunged on their chests flat as boards. The winner smiled, a spontaneous, little-girl smile, for just a moment before turning and giving the camera a sultry, over-the-shoulder pout.

A few days elapsed before I heard a mother talking to a friend. She was complaining that her ten-year-old daughter seemed to be going through a phase of crying easily and was often acting tired. She also mentioned proudly to her friend that her daugher was extremely busy and got all *A*s in school. "She has piano lessons Monday, dancing Tuesday, Girl Scouts Wednesday, choir Thursday, and swimming lessons Friday."

The friend suggested that maybe the "phase" was really fatigue on the part of the daughter. "Maybe you should let up on her!"

"But they're all important for her future," the mother objected. "If she's going to get into a top college, she'll need to be good in many activities."

I don't know if the friend ever convinced the mother that her child needed some unscheduled time for herself. I didn't hear the end of the conversation. But I ran through my mind all the week's related incidents: the pornography Heidi had seen because of parental indifference, the preadolescent sex symbols on TV, and the mother's frantic pushing of her daughter to become a superkid. What they had in common, it seemed to me, is the tendency of late twentieth-century parents to emotionally abuse or neglect their children by encouraging them to grow up too fast. Many of today's children are deprived of real childhood and rushed into a false maturity which they're ill-prepared to handle.

What happens when parents don't realize the effects of nonprotection, or when they don't meet their children's basic needs for security and love, perhaps because of major social changes, such as the increasing divorce rate and mothers' increasing employment outside the home?

"Hurried children are forced to take on the physical, psychological and social trappings of adulthood before they are prepared to deal with them," writes David Elkind in *The Hurried Child.* "We dress our children in miniature adult costumes, often with designer labels, we expose them to gratuitous sex and violence, and we expect them to cope with an increasingly bewildering social environment—divorce, single parenthood, homosexuality." [1]

Unlike spoiled children of a generation ago, today's hurried children grow up too fast, pushed by parents in their early years toward many different types of achievement, and exposed to experiences that tax their adaptive capacity. Today's hurried children are stressed by the fear of not achieving early enough, or by being exposed to experiences they're not capable of handling.

Therapists and teachers are increasingly worried about the tendency of parents to push their children too hard, too fast. At least in dress, manner and worldly knowledge, today's children seem to be growing up faster. Rising rates of sexual activity, drug and alcohol use, and suicide among teens and preadolescents support the impression that today's children are less childlike.

Marie Winn writes in *Children Without Childhood* of a "fictional twelve-year-old from New England named Lolita Haze (who) slept with a middle-aged European intellectual named Humbert Humbert and profoundly shocked American sensibilities. It was not so much the idea of an adult having sexual designs on a child that was appalling. It was Lolita herself, unvirginal long before Humbert came upon the scene, Lolita, so knowing, so jaded, so *unchildlike,* who seemed to violate something America held sacred. The book was banned in Boston. Even a sophisticated book reviewer of *The New York Times* called Nabokov's novel 'repulsive' and 'disgusting.'

"No more than a single generation after *Lolita's* publication, Nabokov's vision of American childhood seems prophetic. There is little doubt that school children of the 1980s are more akin to Nabakov's nymphet than to those guileless and innocent creatures with their shiny Mary Janes and pigtails, their scraped knees and trusting ways, that were called children not so long ago." [2]

The desire to push, to *prepare* children is becoming epidemic. Walking through the bookstore a person sees one title after another aimed at parents who want their children to escape childhood. And parents are buying them! One book promises that you, yes *you,* can teach your nongenius baby to read at twelve months, and play chess at eighteen months. (My children's physical incoordination alone at the age would have resulted in their loss of the games.) The books promise that you can teach your twenty-eight month old to write—not just words, but plays and stories. Other books suggest new ways to relentlessly pursue childhood success for your child, to produce a "superkid."

Parents can find authorities who push for early experience in every aspect of life. Some "authorities" propose that in addition to age-appropriate information on sex, explicit activity should be cultivated, like reading and writing, in childhood. In a widely circulated magazine the implication was clear that parents who worry that their children haven't yet come to enjoy the pleasures of sex, should introduce them to "masturbation, sex play with others of either sex or animals, nudity" and vulgar language.

The notion that latent sexuality might wither and decay if parents don't actively encourage their children to pursue sexual pleasure has caused confusion among some parents. People who grew up with sexual experience being the great separator between children and adults may be comfortable with advice such as that given in the report above and take a laissez-faire attitude toward their children, permitting them to watch television or video pornography.

Neil Postman comments in *The Disappearance of Childhood* that by making almost any human experience visible to viewers of any age, television has eliminated the parents' traditional role as guardian of adult secrets. Parental experiences, whether romantic or financial, are no longer hidden.[3]

How do children deal with this push to grow up fast? Can their emotional growth keep up with the rest of their precocity? Psychiatrists recognize that emotions and feelings are the most intricate parts of development. They cannot be hurried. Children who have the intellectual and physical characteristics of adults often don't *feel* like adults.

So what's the harm in pushing kids to excel, to do more earlier, or in permitting them to be exposed to pornography or overt sex? The basic defect in the various schemes to make superkids is that the impetus comes not from the children themselves, but from parents who are driven by their own needs for fulfillment or achievement. These parents are emotionally abusing their children. They are using their children for their own gratification, and the costs can be cruel. Their kids can grow up with a "patchwork" identity. Elkind's book suggests a number of psychological and physical problems that beset "hurried" youth, including school burnout, over-competitiveness, joylessness, depression, drug and alcohol use and a tendency toward self-centeredness.

What about exposing children to explicit sex? Most experts have come to the conclusion that excessive viewing of sex and violence on TV and in movies is harmful for a variety of reasons. Pornography and explicit sex as presented in the media usually suggest that sex is impersonal, mechanical, often violent, and usually devoid of real commitment and love. Children, who have no basis for knowing better, believe that sex is hostile and that people are used for personal gratification.

When children see their parents watching and enjoying pornography, they believe this is acceptable behavior. According to the media, sex is exploitation of others and that means you are either a victim or an exploiter. Parents who permit their children to see sexual activity presented in this manner are guilty of emotional maltreatment, and the consequences of their actions should be pointed out to them.

Crimes of the Heart

As a social worker, one of the modern-day forms of emotional abuse of which I'm most painfully aware is the situation whereby, because of separation, divorce or remarriage, a child is either fought for by both parents, or, what's even sadder, rejected by both.

At the time I write this chapter, I'm trying to help put back together the lives of two little girls who are wanted by neither of their parents. Mother pretty much walked out of everyone's life when Trudy was two and Marsha was five. That was six years ago. The girls have no idea where their mother is now; she'd promised to come see them last summer, but never showed up. The girls' father, the manager of a large business, is financially comfortable. For the last two or three years he has paid a couple with whom he's acquainted to care for the girls. During that time he has seen them infrequently. "My visits seem to upset them," he explained to me.

When I asked why he had arranged for others to care for the children, not only during the day but also during the nights when he is home, he looked rather sheepish. "The woman I'm living with doesn't get along with them. She doesn't like them, and they don't like her. Those kids broke me up with the girlfriend I had before, and I didn't want it to happen again."

After one visit I showed him the legal document used for parental relinquishment. He was ready to sign it on the spot. "They deserve someone who will take care of them," he said. The seriousness and finality of what he was ready to do didn't seem to bother him. I tried to explain what this would do to his daughters, discovering that no one in all the world, neither their mother nor their father, wanted them. "Burden" was a word he used often to describe his children and, from what he told me, they were already fully aware that was how he felt about them. These are throwaway children, set out on the curb to be picked up by someone else.

Following our talk, I asked the father to think hard about several questions before making a decision. I didn't sleep much that night. How should I advise him? On the one hand, while he had psychologically abandoned the children years earlier, he had maintained a sporadic contact and never explicitly told them, "I don't want you in my life. You're a burden and a bother, and I'm better off without you." Which was worse, the limbo they presently lived in or the blow of hearing from their father that they were out of his life forever.[2] The latter choice offered them a second chance at life through adoption. These children needed that chance.

It's not going to be easy. The eleven-year old daughter is angry and acts out in school and with friends. I worry about her, but I worry even more about her seven-year-old sister. She is withdrawn and shows many signs of an attachment disorder. The people who adopt these girls will need to be strong, patient, resourceful parents, willing to pay in dollars for therapy and in pain for some tough times they all will undoubtedly face.

Soon after the girls' father called me. He said that the night before, over the phone, he'd told his children that he's planning to give them up for adoption. They had called him back later in the evening, he said.

"They were crying. They were crying and angry and tried to lay a guilt trip on me. They wanted to know why I was doing this to them. *You* understand, don't you?" He seemed to plead for one person to approve of his actions.

Though I told him it will probably be better for his daughters in the long run, since he has no desire or intention of improving his relationship with them, the words were hard to get out. He is guilty of emotionally abusing his children at the most basic level. Instead of protecting and loving his children, he is disposing of them.

In addition, every social worker who deals with separated families is familiar with the opposite scenario, a situation wherein both parents demand child custody. Bitter custody fights or kidnapping of children by noncustodial parents make headlines and heart-wrenching TV specials. The tactics used by parents at such times can only be called emotional abuse. Consider the following example.

John had left his wife after years of infidelity on her part. He had always been largely responsible for their young sons' physical and emotional care, and at the time of the divorce, the maternal grandparents agreed that John would be better able to care for their grandsons. Custody was awarded to John and for a time all went well. But then the boys began showing symptoms of the emotional abuse and neglect they had suffered at the hands of their mother before the divorce. Night terrors, restlessness, bedwetting and other symptoms indicated that the boys needed help, and John arranged for counseling. Brett, three, and Jeff, eight, seemed to adjust when, a year later, John married a young widow.

About that time, Marty, the boys' mother, moved in with a man who beat her regularly and refused to work. Marty's phone calls to her sons left them increasingly upset and their behavior after visits with her was disastrous. She begged the boys, especially Jeff, to come and live with her. During the visits and phone calls, she told them in graphic detail about the brutal beatings she received from her boyfriend, and she told Jeff that if he really loved her, he'd ask his dad to let him come back and live with her. "I need you, Jeff," she told him repeatedly.

John and his new wife worried about the possibility of physical as well as emotional abuse to their boys during visits to Marty and her boyfriend, and they began discussing how they could minimize the dangers. About this time Jeff's grades mysteriously began plummeting and John asked for a conference with his teacher.

"Jeff is showing signs of guilt and anxiety," she told his father. "He feels responsible for his mother, and from what he's told me, he thinks she can't get along without him."

What Jeff's mother was doing was unquestionably emotional abuse. As outlined earlier, the expectation that children must meet parental needs, regardless of the cost to children, is destructive and totally unfair. "Come take care of me, I need you," was the message Jeff heard from his mother. He looked around at his father, stepmother and brother, and decided they didn't need him as much as his mother did. He felt guilty and anxious, as his teacher observed, for being loved and protected by his father. He was vulnerable, exploitable, and actively working toward being moved back home so that he could care for his mother.

Experts find that in today's society single-women parents depend on their children for emotional support in a way unknown in previous generations. Whether the custodial parent or not, as in Jeff's case, many divorced mothers use their children as therapists and confidantes, and they expect their children to deal with their stresses and feelings of low self-esteem. As part of the process, one parent often denigrates the other and blames the ex-spouse for everything that's wrong at the present time. The child who probably loves both parents is left feeling torn and pushed to choose between the parent who is "right" or the one who's "wrong", between the one who is "good" or the one who is "bad". The conflict is just one of the forms emotional abuse takes among late twentieth-century parents.

Latchkey and Day Care Neglect

Another form of emotional and physical neglect inflicted upon contemporary children is due to the fact that nearly twenty million American mothers with children under eighteen now work outside the home. These women, who work for economic necessity and/or for personal fulfillment, have drastically changed the way in which children were raised a generation or two ago. Before World War I, women were not especially prominent in the U.S. work force. Fewer divorces meant more mothers staying at home with their young children. The extended family was more available in those less-mobile days. If mothers did work outside the home, an aunt or grandmother often would be responsible for child care.

During World War II, women entered the work force in record numbers. Many mothers, whose husbands were off fighting the enemy, welcomed the opportunity to escape for several hours a day the demands of being full-time mothers *and* fathers. When the war was over and men returned to their work, many women stayed on as a permanent part of the work force. Since then, the rate at which married women work in the labor force has risen. In 1980, the percentage passed fifty percent for the first time. For many of these women, affordable, in-home child care is unavailable, and the choice is between parental unemployment or lack of child supervision. It is estimated that there are 32,000 preschoolers without daytime supervision and over two million latchkey or school-age children left alone several hours a day.[4]

This trend, probably irreversible, has led to hundreds of studies and observations on the effect of working mothers on individual children and on the family in general. Until recently, vociferous and differing opinions from various quarters did little to settle the important questions that parents and others have about the good and bad results of mothers' employment. Debate over the harmfulness of mothers—and fathers—leaving children first at day care centers, then alone as latchkey children, has raged for years.

Conclusions are beginning to emerge from reputable researchers. Some of their findings may be comforting to parents who depend on day care centers and on their children who are left alone while the parents are at work. Other findings are disquieting and suggest the potential for emotional abuse and neglect of our children.

First, the good news. Numerous studies indicate that a mother's employment can have positive effects on her children. Children of employed women tend to be more independent and responsible than children of nonemployed women.

When the mother of latchkey or day care children enjoys her work and feels good about herself and what she's doing, her self-esteem spills over and raises the self-esteem of her children. They understand that women have career choices and aspirations, and can be financially independent. Her children, especially her daughters, shouldn't feel the urge to rush into early and loveless marriages because they see that as the only means for a woman to support herself. Children with working mothers view women as vital, interesting people with concerns that extend further than the family circle.

But not all children of working mothers have positive experiences. What makes day care or self-care happy and productive for some and less so for others seems to depend a great deal on the unique personality of each child. Some kids inherently seem to better handle the stress of being alone, the fears and loneliness, than do others.

The Handbook for Latchkey Children and Their Parents, by Lynette and Thomas Long, explains that "Because of the lack of presence of an adult, feelings of fear are more frequent and enduring for latchkey children than for children who are under continuous adult care. For the latchkey child feelings of fear are also experienced more frequently because of their own hypersensitivity to household noises, the impact of extended hours of watching television, the communication of possible dangers passed on to them by concerned parents, the real dangers of the latchkey situation, and the fact that children simply feel more vulnerable when alone. The fears of latchkey children are also felt for longer periods of time . . . (they) don't have the benefit of having a fear immediately relieved" (by a caretaker).[5]

Usually the fears are imaginary, but occasionally they're real. My community has been saddened by the accidental death and disfigurement of children left to their own devices who started a disastrous fire. Latchkey children are more vulnerable to the results of accidents or mischief caused by boredom, to the threat of fire, explosion or other natural disasters, to the threat of violence such as burglaries, and to the psychological dangers from obscene or mysterious phone calls, knocks at the door, and so on.

These dangers are only a small part of the stresses faced by latchkey children. They are challenged by events and situations that would make their grandparents shake their heads in disbelief. Many latchkey children are exposed to excessive amounts of TV with its steady diet of sex, violence and egocentricism. Many are trying to cope with other confusion in their lives— parental divorce or separation, economic uncertainty and their perception of being either a burden or the parental confidante.

Social observers such as Dr. Elkind believe that these stresses are simply too much for many children, and when parents disregard these effects on their offspring, they emotionally neglect them. For today's parents faced with a world that is, for many, changing too fast, much of life seems to be out of their control. In their study of latchkey children, Drs. Lynette and Thomas Long found that parents seek to reduce their stress at home by hurrying children to grow up or by treating them as adults.

"Many latchkey parents select self-care for their children precisely to reduce parental stress. It is not simply the cost of child care or the lack of a suitable child-care facility that leads many parents to decide in favor of a latchkey arrangement, but the stress caused by the combined pressure of cost, facility, transportation, and the confining schedule that out-of-home care imposes. These parents seem willing to accept the burden of guilt a latchkey arrangement exacts in favor of release from other stressors, especially when convenient, inexpensive, adult-supervised care arrangements are not available within easy walking distance . . ."

Other child experts believe that the effects of "latchkeyism" extend beyond problems found within the child or home. They see the feelings of alienation, boredom and loneliness extending to academic failure, violence, vandalism and experimentation with alcohol and drugs. Several law enforcement officers I have visited report seeing more and more latchkey or unsupervised children in trouble, beginning with elementary-age kids who break and enter or vandalize neighborhood property.

The latchkey experience need not be a horrible and abusive period for children. Parents can and do find ways to minimize risks and offer comfort to lonely and bored children. Too often, however, children are emotional casualties of their parents' rushing them into responsibility that they're not ready to handle.

In what Mt. Sinai Hospital of Chicago describes as the first pediatric program of its kind, abused, neglected and emotionally troubled children will have their own ward. Dr. Howard Levy, chairman of the pediatrics department who helped develop the program, said children appropriate for treatment include latchkey kids who have been emotionally traumatized from their experiences. Obviously, the problem is being taken seriously by professionals.

One suggestion for parents concerned about their children spending after school hours alone is to leave a cassette tape with a prerecorded message for them to play after returning from school. The tape might include a reassuring message such as "I love you", or instructions for chores or other information. Parents who cannot themselves call to make sure children have made it home safely from school can arrange for a neighbor or nearby friend to call the child at the same time each day.

One mother has put together a special phone book for her seven-year-old to use during the hour he is left unattended each day. On separate pages, she has pictures of firemen, police, the family doctor and others her son might want to call. Under each picture she has clearly written appropriate telephone numbers.

Day Care Dangers

What about day care? The controversy rages on. Many specialists believe that children who attend a *quality* (emphasis on quality) program and are welcomed back home by affectionate, time-sharing parents will probably do all right. Parents cannot, however, blithely drop their kids at any day care door and expect the staff to meet their children's needs.

I found no authority who would state without qualification that eight or more hours in day care could be in children's best interests. William and Wendy Dreskin, authors of *The Day Care Decision: What's Best for Your Child,* write "For two years we watched day care children in our own preschool/day care center respond to the stress of eight to ten hours a day of separation from there parents with tears, anger, withdrawal, or profound sadness, and we found to our dismay, that there was nothing in our own affection and caring for these children that would erase this sense of abandonment. We came to realize that the amount of separation—the number of hours a day spent away from parents—is a critical factor." [6]

What may harm children in day care more than the dangers inherent in self care is the common multiplicity of care providers. At the very time in a child's life when continuity and stability are most needed, babies and very young children are usually the wards of all the caretakers. When one particular caretaker is assigned to particular children, as is the case in some progressive centers, the high rate of employee turnover mitigates against that happy arrangement lasting very long. As a result, an intimate, one-to-one relationship between the child and substitute caregiver is seldom established except in the best (and most expensive) of day care centers.

In ordinary family life there is usually some awareness of the changing moods and needs of the child; but this is not the case in most institutions wherein changing caretakers respond in varied ways to what they see, *if* and *when* they see it. Just when kids most need to be understood, protected and reassured, they are more likely to be overlooked or handled without empathy or understanding.

One of the most critical voices raised against the negative effects of day care for babies and toddlers comes from Dr. Burton L. White, considered by many to be America's foremost expert on early childhood. In his position as Project Director of Harvard University's Preschool Project, he has studied hundreds of babies for thousands of hours, and he arrived at the conclusion that the first three years of life are critical in a child's development. His words are blunt. ". . . we came to believe that the informal education that families provide for their children makes more of an impact on a child's total educational development than the formal educational system. If a family does its job well, the professional can then provide effective training. If not, there may be little the professional can do to save the child from mediocrity. This grim assessment is a direct conclusion from the findings of thousands of programs in remedial education such as Head Start and Follow Through projects." [7]

His opinions regarding the effects of day care on children have made some parents and educators angry, but he steadfastly defends them. Refusing to give specific advice on what working parents should do about child care, he confines his observations to conclusions drawn after studying babies and toddlers for over twenty years.

It is his opinion that eight or more hours of day care a day, five days a week, cannot possibly be as beneficial to the child's development as being home for the first three years. The exception would be those stressful homes where financial hardship, alcoholism or other problems might make a nurturing environment unlikely.

Child care workers, even the best, Dr. White explains, cannot possibly react to the achievements of babies and toddlers with the same excitement and intensity of a parent. They have seen countless children stand up, walk or climb for the first time. They're just not going to genuinely "go bananas" over these milestones with the enthusiasm of a parent. Children deserve the sense of being totally precious and irreplaceable, something hard to come by in a center caring for a dozen or more children.

Few women who work can afford the ideal in day care (one constant companion who is capable of both warmth and discipline, living in the child's home and responsible only for that child and brothers and sisters). There are no indications that in the future the likelihood of this rosy picture will improve. Pushing children into adult experience does not make then precociously mature, but may lead them to cling to childhood all through their lives.

Dr. John Bowlby, whose attachment research has been described, has been and still is at the center of controversy regarding conflicting demands of the child and of the mother's needs for employment. In an interview published in *Psychology Today,* he explained his position as simply trying to understand, not to advise. "All the evidence is that children prosper if they have a couple of parents with whom they live and the home is a stable, predictable one. Now, if you can arrange for a child to be cared for by some motherly person whom the child knows and feels secure with, if it's a regular routine . . . then, okay. Day nurseries—well, it's a very rare day nursery that gives enough care. I'm not saying it's impossible, but it's rare and it's expensive. And if you can't make stable arrangements, then you're going to have emotional difficulties with the child and a lot of unhappiness." [8]

He admits finding the kind of care he advocates difficult, if not impossible, for some. Many parents with whom I work reply bitterly when they hear comments such as his. They are having a hard time arranging for mediocre care, and finding a granny-type caretaker such as Dr. Bowlby advocates is as likely as finding a fairy godmother to drop by to babysit.

It may be a cliche, but it still bears repeating. The way we spend our time reveals what—or whom—we care most about.

In the past, parents tried to *protect* children from ugly truths about adult life; now they prepare them for unhappiness, even sexual trauma and exploitation. Partly due to social changes, parents have pushed their children into being equals or better, sharing responsibility, making decisions and going through every seamy fact of life with them.

Childhood should be special. While no parent need become a slave to the demands of his child, a child's well-being must be paramount. If that is at the cost of some parental ambitions, so be it. Children deserve better than what they are getting in many modern homes today. Pushing them into adult experience does not make them precociously mature, but may lead them to cling to childhood throughout their lives.

Chapter Seven

"I'm the Baddest Kid"

Effects of Emotional Maltreatment

From the previous chapters the reader is already familiar with many presumed effects of emotional maltreatment. In discussing abuse and neglect, *cause* and *effect* are not black-and-white, clear-cut entities. The title of E. Milling Kinard's article, "Child Abuse and Depression: Cause or Consequence?"[1] exemplifies the chicken-or-the-egg? nature of the problem. The complex intertwining of cause and effect can be noted in the lives of the children suffering the effects of emotional abuse whose case studies are examined in this chapter.

Jamie—A Victim of Psychosocial Dwarfism

Jamie is a ten-year-old youngster currently in a residential treatment facility. He lived with us for a time when our family was an assessment home for children considered to be at high risk for regular foster care.

Removed from his home several times during the course of his short life because of evidence suggesting abuse and/or neglect, Jamie was in the custody of the child welfare agency when he was placed with us. His history indicates probable abuse dating back to early infancy, as well as alarming developmental deviations and delays. The earliest evaluation available to me was performed when Jamie was eighteen months old. At that time, his pediatrician described him as being "irritable, withdrawn, and an extremely immature child who had multiple bruises on his chest and head. X-rays revealed a healed bone fracture in one arm that had occurred at about two months of age. At that time, the diagnosis was made of "psychomotor retardation secondary to maternal deprivation and failure to thrive." A neurological exam showed his bone age to be in the three-to-six month range. As is typical with failure-to-thrive babies, after only seven days in the hospital, he put on weight and appeared less irritable, and more responsive to nurses. In the words of one of his nurses, he gained weight and seemed more "normal."

During the mother's infrequent visits to the hospital, the staff noted her volatile temper, as well as the lack of mutual attachment behaviors between her and her son. I wondered if Jamie had been born with a congenitally "difficult" temperament as described in Chapter Four. This guess was confirmed by records indicating that from birth, he had considerable difficulty in sleeping and eating, vomiting frequently with no underlying physiological problem discovered. He was described by professionals, as well as his mother, as never being a "cuddly baby." He seemed to be one of those infants whose irritability and crying helped push parents beyond their threshhold of violence. For parents such as Jamie's, who already had a high potential for neglect and abuse, a difficult infant can precipitate neglect or vicious attacks.

Jamie did not walk or talk until he was nearly three. By this time, he was receiving Dexadrine in rather massive dosages, after having been diagnosed by another pediatrician as suffering from minimal brain dysfunction. At age two, he was treated at various times for burns to his legs, scrotum and thighs, described as "accidents," and at age three, after multiple bruises to head, arms and chest, he was placed briefly in foster care. His bedwetting appeared to have precipitated several beatings on the part of his parents, but less well-documented was the emotional neglect that caused his deprivational or psychosocial dwarfism.

At age five when he began kindergarten, Jamie's behavior caused grave concern to his teachers, and he began receiving large dosages of Ritalin. This did not prevent him from continuing to exhibit abuse-inviting behaviors. The mother was reported to have rubbed Jamie's face in the rug on which he had deliberately wet and a new regimen of medication was tried, again with little success.

By this time, Jamie's medical records showed clear evidence of psychosocial dwarfism. At age eight and one-half, he weighed only thirty-five pounds and his height was forty-one inches. His skull circumference was that of a three-year-old.

School could only be described as chaotic for Jamie, his teachers and classmates. He was found foraging for food in school dumpsters and threw incredible temper tantrums that prevented his teacher from relating to others in the classroom. He wanted to be cuddled by his teacher and held close, begging for reassurance that he was cared for; then paradoxically, (in the words of his classmates) he threw "fits," which left them scared and disgusted.

When he came to live with us at age nine, he was smaller by far than our average-sized five year old. His behaviors, including urinating on himself and in other unsuitable places, defecating many times a day in his underwear, and ceaselessly wandering the house during the night in search of food or adventure, did not make for a peaceful time when he lived with us. While in school, Jamie showed amazing mood swings. He would alternate between being a little boy who wanted to be held like a toddler, and behaving like a kicking, spitting, biting imp who destroyed property, even things he treasured, all the while laughing sardonically.

It's no wonder a teacher's aide, unbeknownst to us, decided Jamie was possessed, and conducted an exorcism on him one Sunday while our family enjoyed a bit of respite. When the earnest young fellow returned Jamie to us that evening, he assured us that Jamie would have no more problems, that the devil had been driven out of him. When later that night Jamie went into one of his colossal tantrums and tried to bite me, I wished a guarantee had been part of the package.

It didn't take more than a few days to see that even with the most skilled of foster parents, Jamie could not function in a normal home. The effects of years of emotional and physical abuse and neglect, combined with a congenitally difficult temperament, had taken their toll. He was a little boy—in every sense—who was out of control. He had repeatedly been told that he was responsible for his mother's nervous breakdown, his father's drinking and abusive episodes, and his grandmother's heart attack. He believed all of this and talked about being the "baddest boy" who had ever lived. At times he seemed to try to live up to that expectation. Depression and deprivational dwarfism were diagnosed after the decision was made to send Jamie for an out-of-state pediatric evaluation.

Deprivational or psychosocial dwarfism, a little-known syndrome, may be more common than people realize. A Denver pediatrician told me that he has seen many children who are considered merely "small for their age" whom he strongly suspects suffer from being deprived of love, and who, after better testing, are diagnosed as having psychosocial dwarfism (PSD).

Researchers believe that when children are not given the love they need, emotional and physical disturbances in the child nearly always occur to some degree. At first the disturbance is registered in the higher, more-developed brain centers. Then, it is theorized, the more primitive part of the brain, the hypothalamus, is affected, which, in turn, regulates the pituitary or "master gland" of the endocrine system. When the growth hormone released by the pituitary, somatotropin, is not produced in sufficient quantities, the result is a stunted child.

Experts, such as Dr. Nancy Hopwood and her associates, believe that environmentally induced growth retardation, as with Jamie, is probably the most common cause of deviant growth in infants and children in the U.S. All too often, however, the small stature and lack of normal bone growth is attributed to other reasons. In a study of 35 children who were diagnosed as having psychosocial dwarfism (PSD), Hopwood and her associate found that initially many families of the affected children presented a facade of stability and appeared nurturing, a factor that often had delayed the correct diagnosis.[2]

Although a complex relationship exists between brain function and release of the growth hormone somatotropin, the theory outlined above seems to be validated by the fact that a child who is dwarfed due to emotional neglect can make rapid growth gains when placed in a more nurturing environment. That is exactly what happened when Jamie lived with us. His medical record shows a weight gain of six pounds after three weeks with us, and a subsequent height spurt soon after. Apparently, when a child with PSD receives stimulation and affection, the somatotropin level rises remarkably, and sudden growth results.[3]

Other scientists have studied the relationship between sleeping patterns and the release of the growth hormone. Most somatotropin is released into the bloodstream during the sleep stage when higher brain centers are least active. Since most victims of PSD have very irregular sleep, it is possible that because of their emotional deficits, these babies or children aren't able to reach that stage of sleep. Research on diagnosed PSD children who have later received proper nurturing shows that when hormonal growth resumes, so does a normal sleeping pattern.

Jamie's experiences at home are largely surmised. As is the case with most children who are diagnosed as having PSD, Jamie was not initially brought for medical evaluation by his family, but by protective services. The child's record shows a long history of endeavors by the father to undermine the mother's attempts at discipline. Unfortunately, the harsh punishment inflicted upon Jamie seems to be the only attention of any kind he received at home. It is not surprising that some of his irritability and dangerous behaviors were designed to get someone, anyone, to notice him.

Both of Jamie's parents had themselves experienced early parental loss. The father's parents both died when he was a young teenager, and the mother was abandoned at age three by her own mother with no contact whatsoever after that time. Remembering Harlow's deprived baby monkeys who were later unable to be adequate mothers, one wonders if Jamie's mother was not as much a victim of emotional abuse as is her son.

Jamie's mother became pregnant with an older brother when she was in high school, and the couple then married. Shortly after that child's birth, Jamie was conceived. Several other children were born to the couple, who stayed together off and on throughout a rocky marriage. Although periodically beaten by her husband, Jamie's mother stayed dependent on him and refused offers to continue her high school education or to obtain employment that might have given her some positive feelings about herself.

At the present time, Jamie's parents seem to actively undermine his progress in the residential treatment facility. He is, for example, promised visits that never materialize because his parents "forget" to come. During infrequent telephone calls, he is subjected to harangues regarding how bad he has been. Jamie's progress is slow. He continues to be encopretic (incontinent), although his feces-smearing has decreased somewhat.

Psychological and neurological testing has revealed no evidence of an organic brain dysfunction. It was shown, however, that Jamie cannot function well with ambiguity, anger, or frustration. As with many victims of child abuse, Jamie shows a short attention span and poor impulse control. At times he seems unable to distinguish fantasy from reality.

Jamie's fantasies are revealing. While living with us, he talked about wishing he were a bear or a reindeer because they could sleep much of the year. He also expressed the desire to be a police officer when he grew up. When I asked him what he'd do if he were a policeman, he said, "I'd lock up bad people, like me." Even after a year of treatment, Jamie sees himself as a bad person, one who is to blame for the dysfunction in his family. He sees his placement at the treatment facility as a punishment for the bad things he's done and the bad person he is.

A psychiatric evaluation indicates Jamie would require a minimum of three years treatment at the facility where he has been placed. The psychiatrist believes that, given Jamie's regressive and immature behaviors and his interpersonal and cognitive delays, allowing this ten-year-old to operate at a five or six-year-old level might permit him to master the usual expectations for children of that age in a group setting. The doctor suggested that, rather than restraining Jamie when he is out of control, kicking, and biting, to hold him tightly, thus providing him with the close nurturing that he lacked as an angry, unlovable infant and toddler.

What will happen to Jamie? Some nights when I lie awake from too much coffee, I wonder what will ever become of him. Of what is this child capable? He appears to have no conscience, no remorse, no impulse control, but only a boundless anger at the world.

I believe that when a person cannot talk about the cruelty endured as a child because it was experienced so early that it began before memory, then the child demonstrates the cruelty. Some are cruel to others; some become self-destructive. Because of emotional abuse and neglect, how many other children like Jamie live as time bombs, ticking off the months or years until they explode with rage at themselves or society?

Symptoms and Behavior Related to Psychosocial Dwarfism

Researchers have reported a bizarre array of symptoms and behaviors associated with children diagnosed as having PSD. By far the most common symptom is an unusual eating pattern. Eighty-six per cent of PSD children studied by Hopwood and Becker were polyphagic (overeaters). These children generally had voracious appetites, and would eat nonfood items such as dirt, paper, crayons and dog food. Reports of these children eating unusual or excessive amounts of food were common (a jar of mayonnaise, two whole pies, a box of cinnamon, etc.) Abdominal distension, vomiting and diarrhea often followed such ingestion. Parents of the children studied reportedly had tried to control their children's abnormal eating, but were often outwitted by their children who got up at night to raid the kitchen or who stole and begged food from other people. Many of these children liked to play in the kitchen and talked animatedly about food. Concern with food appeared to be more significant to them than family relationships, toys, or other normal preoccupations.

A second group of regressive behaviors in the children studied included enuresis (bedwetting) or, drinking from the toilet, fishbowl or other unsuitable places. Half the children studied showed temper tantrums, but many would also withdraw periodically and stare at the floor or sit in one spot for an extended time. Of primary concern to many parents was the nighttime wandering of their children. Insensitivity to pain, self-mutilation, and hyperactivity were reported in many of these children. Often, as with Jamie, many of these symptoms were present in the same child.

Physically, these children appear much younger than their chronological ages. They have head circumferences, body proportions and faces that make them appear younger than they are. Diagnostic clues, other than physical signs such as head circumference, bone maturation and blood lipids, include external factors such as maternal depression, marital conflict, and hostile or emotionally absent parents. Physical abuse between parents and/or parents and child, parental childhood deprivation and multiple family stresses (unemployment, financial difficulty, chronic illness, drug or alcohol abuse) were commonly found in the backgrounds of the children studied. In all cases, poor communication was present between parents. Usually one or both parents denied any problem regarding their child's abnormal size. Scapegoating the child, blaming and manipulating through guilt were found in a large number of PSD families.

Often the terms nonorganic failure-to-thrive and psychosocial dwarfism are used interchangeably. While family pathology is similar in both conditions, several clinical features differ.

FTT symptoms are usually present to the pediatrician before the age of two. The infant's abnormally low weight for age, muscle wasting and loose folds of skin are the most prominent physical symptoms. Although linear growth may be slightly reduced, it is not a major feature. Behavior is usually withdrawn and apathetic.

The striking feature of children diagnosed as PSD is extremely short stature. Although dwarfed, these children do not look particularly malnourished. The symptoms, in addition to the behavior earlier described, are usually present between the ages of two and fifteen.

Psychiatrists and endocrinologists puzzle over why, in families with similar pathology, some children may develop FTT in infancy and others develop PSD at a later age. Jamie may be very unusual in that he showed both conditions at appropriate ages. Dr. Kim Oates believes that PSD constitutes a subgroup within the nonorganic FTT syndrome and that both conditions are reversible to some degree, if treated in time.[4]

Experts who are familiar with these families are pessimistic that therapy can cause enough change to permit the child to grow normally. Evidently, a pathology severe enough to shut down a child's natural growth is very resistive to change. As in the case with Jamie's family, the parents often deny the existence of any problem except for those caused by interfering professionals. They may refuse any proffered help toward change.

Another reason these families seldom become functional long enough for the child to grow is the insufficiency of skilled mental health workers. Those families willing to accept help usually are unable to pay for the type of family therapy needed, even if it is available.

Deprivational or psychosocial dwarfism is an extreme example of how withholding love and nurturing can affect a child's physical growth. Because symptoms are so obvious and measurable, PSD can be better researched than more subtle forms of neglect. Perhaps in the future children whose symptoms are less extreme will be recognized as also suffering from the effects of deprivation. These children may be small and weak, frequently sick, or show less severe forms of the behavioral disturbances described. Babies who show no strong vocal reactions to mother's inappropriate actions, who avert their gaze or shut down in sleep-like states may be slipping into psychosocial dwarfism. The extreme defensive state of withdrawal, depression and physiological shutdown can be signalling the onset of not only emotional, but physical stunting as well.

Some researchers theorize that eating disorders of adolescence, such as anorexia and bulimia, are caused by emotional deprivation in childhood. Whether or not this is found to be true, the fact remains that for younger children, a loving environment is not something "extra". Not only their emotional, but their physical development, depends on warmth and acceptance.

Penny—A Victim of Self-Mutilation

Trichotillomania is the word used by experts to describe one of the forms of self-mutilation Penny has inflicted on herself. *Sick* is what casual observers call the scars that cover Penny's arms and hands. Lumpy, unnatural bumps flesh over the acid and cigarette burns, razor slices, jabbed glass and pencil eraser abrasions that cover her thin arms.

Scars that blemish the rest of her young body are hidden by jeans and a T-shirt that announces her sexual availability. Only a few facial wounds— mostly healed—and her arms reveal the addiction she has to hurting herself. Penny looks at the scars that map her life and in a matter-of-fact voice she recalls what prompted each one.

Penny is well-known to emergency room personnel. She has been admitted countless times to the lockup ward and intensive care unit in various hospitals for slashed muscles, drug overdoses and third-degree burns. Her illness is not rare, and is seen more and more frequently by social workers and medical professionals. Although the incomprehensible self-punishment is seen in children still in elementary school, it is most common in young adults. The tools that she and others like herself use to inflict injury to themselves include razors, broken glass, burning paper taped to skin, boiling water, their own fists, fingernails and teeth, and of course, chemicals that burn, poison or oversedate. The reasons for the mutilations usually involve emotional neglect. Parents of these self-mutilators are rarely aware of the extent of their children's unhappiness.

If you ask Penny why she hurts herself so badly, so often, she can rattle off psychoanalytical reasons. She doesn't really know why. She says she doesn't want to die, but is addicted to hurting herself and gains a perverse pleasure from doing so.

Self-abuse addicts calculate exactly how far they can go toward the brink of death without falling over. They know exactly how many drugs to take to land in a hospital ICU for 24 or 72 hours, depending on the length of stay they want. They learn with a precision that makes pharmacologists marvel, what combinations of medications will erupt in their bodies. They know what causes second or third degree burns, depending on what they're wanting. They pore over *Merck Manuals* and deliberate about what prescriptions to forge on stolen pads.

Penny admits that none of this makes any sense. "I'm afraid of my feelings," she says. "I know what I'm doing can kill me if I figure times or injuries wrong. But I can't help myself. Hospitals are the only place I feel safe."

She describes herself as a "professional patient." "That's the only place I'm secure. That's worth the strange looks and questions the nurses and doctors ask me. I can deal with the questions. It's my feelings I can't handle."

She picks at one of the countless scars on her hands. "When I'm concentrating on getting to the E.R. to be stitched up or have my stomach pumped, I don't feel lonely. Everyone is paying attention to me. I tell myself that this is the last time, that I'll quit hurting myself, but I know deep down that I can't stop."

According to psychiatrists, the self-mutilation disorder primarily affects women. Many suffer from various eating disorders as well, and have histories of sexual trauma. They often begin their self-mutilation by cutting or tatooing their breasts, then go on to more severe and obvious self-injuries.

People unfamiliar with the syndrome see it as an extreme plea for attention. In reality, many victims hide their injuries and try to treat themselves. These women find a tension release with the experience of pain, and even promise themselves rewards of future injuries.

Penny has burned herself with chemicals, swallowing batteries and waiting for the acid to spread within her stomach. She constantly visualizes cutting herself. She reports "I think before cutting about the control I have when I get taken to the E.R. The relief floods over me. I only hope I can stop for good before I accidentally kill myself someday."

Patricia, A Victim of Depression

Although no single factor has been identified as leading to childhood or adult depression, research evidence indicates that being abused and/or having depressed parents, particularly mothers, increases the likelihood of its development.

Martin Seligmann has advanced a theory of depression as "learned helplessness," an explanation that holds credibility in exploring depression in maltreated children. Seligmann's research shows that when people believe their actions make no difference—certainly the case with many abused children—they feel helpless, then depressed.[5] Patricia's case study shows how learned helplessness led to the onset of depressive symptoms.

Patricia, the daughter of a tough, no-nonsense professional man and his homemaker wife, had been observed by teachers to have a short attention span while in kindergarten. In elementary school, she was very intelligent and managed to get good grades in spite of a time-limited ability to concentrate. Teachers liked her and she was popular with friends as well.

At home, however, life was not so pleasant. Her parents were impatient and highly critical of her because she was dreamy and forgetful. The increasing tension began to take its toll in school and, at age eight, a clinical evaluation was performed. Patricia's parents were hostile to her during the evaluation and reported nail-tearing, frequent bed-wetting and an increasing tendency toward distractibility.

Recommendations that her parents lighten up on criticism and lavish more praise and positive attention on Patricia were scorned by the father and ignored by the mother. Her symptoms grew worse. Her schoolwork deteriorated and she began showing tics and other nervous mannerisms. Both Patricia and her mother reported that the father became increasingly abusive verbally to his daughter and rejecting of her. He told her he wished she'd never been born, that she was "a loser," and would never amount to anything. Although Patricia's mother did not agree with this treatment, her attempts to stop it were weak and ineffectual.

The harder that Patricia tried to win her father's approval, the worse he reacted to her. While in high school, she determined to raise her grades, and studied far into the night. Anxiety during the tests sabotaged her goal. Because of the stress in her home, she simply could not sustain the effort needed to get good grades. The harder she tried, the more she failed in the eyes of her father. She felt helpless, then increasingly depressed.

Counseling records indicate that at age sixteen, Patricia described herself as always feeling sad and tired, as being incompetent and lazy. She looked and acted defeated with a passive, hang-dog appearance. She had no friends and spent most of her time shut up in her bedroom where she drew morbid pictures dealing with themes of death or violence. She stopped doing any meaningful school work, telling others she knew she'd fail all her classes anyway.

Her father compared Patricia negatively to her younger sister, a daughter who seems to have all the qualities he wanted in Patricia. The girls avoided each other whenever possible, and the younger sister referred to the older as "Weird One" or "Morticia" (characters from The Addams' Family television show). Although Patricia is receiving counseling, the outlook for this depressed young woman is not good.

The experience of emotional deprivation, such as Patricia experienced, seems to be more devastating than actual loss through death or separation of a parent (depending on the type of experiences that follow). While the physical loss of parents can be dealt with by positive relationships with other caregivers, the emotional loss through deprivation or rejection continues unmercilessly through time. Data available from many researchers suggest that emotional deprivation in childhood, rather than loss or separation, will create adult depression.

It would be a foolish oversimplification to imply that parental maltreatment is the only cause of depression, a malady estimated to affect from four to eight million Americans. Like many clinical labels, depression embraces a whole family of disorders. It is not much more specific than "diseases of the skin" which might describe acne or cancer. The term may refer to process depression (hormonally based and/or time-cyclical) or reactive depression (caused by separation from loved ones, personal failure, growing old, and so on). The common denominator of these experiences is the belief in one's own helplessness.

The behavioral phenomenon of learned helplessness, like so many other scientific findings, was stumbled upon by Seligman and his associates while they were using dogs and traumatic shock to test a learning theory. As part of the test, they strapped dogs into a Pavlovian harness and electrically shocked them to the point of trauma, but not to physical damage. Later, the dogs were expected to learn to escape shock by jumping over a barrier separating a two-compartment shuttle-box. This would happen ordinarily with "naive" dogs not having prior experience as Seligman's subjects.

But these dogs had already experienced shock over which they had no control. They did not try to escape, but instead passively took as much shock as the researchers delivered. After initially believing that the trauma (shock) itself caused the apathy, the scientists theorized that it was instead, the experience of having no control over the trauma. Additional testing showed that if animals are given the chance to control or modify trauma by their responses, they do not act helpless. The dogs who gave up and made no attempt to get away were the animals given uncontrollable shock. These dogs had learned that their actions made no difference, and, apparently, they inferred that they were helpless.

Emotionally abused children are much like Seligman's subjects in that regard. They have learned their efforts to please parents make no difference. They perceive all experiences as failures. They see themselves as incompetent and powerless, vulnerable to the whims or tyranny of the abusive parent.

Sometimes depression among emotionally abused children is so severe that suicide appears to be the only escape. Two psychiatrists studied the cases of sixteen suicidal children between the ages of two and five, and they discovered that what seems to be unthinkable—babes in arms trying to kill themselves—does happen.[6] Thirteen of the sixteen had tried to commit suicide more than once—by ingesting household chemicals or prescription drugs which they knew to be dangerous, running into heavy traffic, or jumping from high places.

When compared to sixteen control group youngsters, (children who suffered from such symptoms as hyperactivity or unmanageable behavior), the suicidal children showed more depressive symptoms. They were more likely to have tried running away and displayed more aggressive behavior toward themselves. Even though the children were very young, few of them cried or showed common reactions to pain after their suicide attempts.

In the subsequent therapy, almost all of them expressed profound feelings of abandonment and despair. Most parents of these children admitted they simply were not wanted.

Other Effects of Maltreatment

The world of emotionally maltreated children is a dangerous and hostile one. Since it is also unpredictable, the child never knows what may provoke rejection or humiliation, and a variety of coping mechanisms are developed to help adapt to his scary environment.

Abused children constantly "check out" the moods of the adults around them. A poignant hypervigilance characterizes many of them. Wary and watchful, they often develop a precocious ability to "read" people. Superficially, they may appear to possess social skills, but a quality of defensiveness underlies any attempts at friendliness.

Professionals working with such children frequently notice their extreme sensitivity to any change in environment. They may "test the waters" by asking an inordinate number of questions or study face and body language for cues. Many therapists have noted the chameleon-like nature of abused children's personalities, their moods and behavior shifting in reaction to nuances of their environment. Living their lives in reaction to adults creates many problems in later life.

Along with a blunting of honest feelings, abused children often inhibit their own activity to avoid notice. If a child's words and actions have met with ridicule, silence becomes preferable to risking punishment. This does not mean that abused children do not have opinions or minds of their own. In an attempt to maintain some integrity and yet not invite abuse, these children often become experts at passive resistance.

Teachers can be frustrated by students who appear to do without actually doing, who say "yes" while doing the opposite. Such children may be showing the effects of abuse, denying and distoring their behaviors. Frequently after the child has "played dumb", teachers are amazed to learn from standardized tests that his potential far exceeds performance.

More than fifty abused children were observed over a three-year period by Dr. Alayne Yates, who then categorized these children into three groups, according to their personality characteristics.[7] The first group, classified as *destructive,* are extraordinarily irritable and angry. They destroy property, injure people and animals, and show little or no remorse. They literally ask to be abused by their caretakers, as was the case with Jamie. After years of verbal and physical abuse, he truly seemed to be deprived without punishment, and begged me to hit him or worse. (I must admit at times my natural impulse was to gladly oblige him.)

Destructive children, such as Jamie, require constant supervision. Since neither their impulse control nor their conscience have developed, they cannot be trusted. In Jamie's case, I learned that lesson within an hour of his arrival in our home. He had by that time pushed out a second-story window screen and taken five-year-old John with him out on the roof.

From there, Jamie began dropping a tape recorder, a children's phonograph and other toys onto the porch below for the pleasure of watching them destroyed.

That destructiveness and untrustworthiness, combined with qualities Jamie shared with other destructive abused children, meant that for the assessment month he lived with us I slept with one eye open and both ears turned up. Many destructive children who are victims of emotional and other abuse show tendencies toward firesetting, daytime enuresis, regressive rages, vandalism, extreme restlessness, including night wanderings, and cruelty to animals or children. With Jamie, firesetting and cruelty to children were not observed.

By itself, play therapy for such individuals does not usually eliminate such symptoms. The damage done to the child is so pervasive that a consistent, highly structured environment simultaneous with other forms of treatment seem to be the child's only hope for a normal life.

The second, and more numerous, group of emotionally abused victims that Dr. Yates identified were the *frightened* children. Most girls tend to fall into this category. While being observed in the hospital setting, most of these children stayed in bed and avoided contact whenever possible. They are more compliant than the destructive group, but more covert in the ways they show their anger. These children are the picky eaters, the compulsive stealers or liars, the children who appear to be doing but don't do. They make cooperative gestures, even saying "yes," while doing the opposite. Most of the foster children placed in our home through the years fell into this classification.

The third group Dr. Yates described as being the most interesting. They are the *private* children who have "precocious ego function in some areas and alarming deficits in others." These children might be almost "spooky" in their ability to "read" others' feelings or thoughts, yet have no attachments to particular people or objects such as a teddy bear or blanket.

These young children (infants to age six) appear pleasant, attractive, and very bright. Even the youngest ones seem to quickly learn hospital routine and be able to predict what will be happening (mealtime or venipuncture, for example) from the barest of cues. These children, hypersensitive to methods of manipulation, learn which nurse can best be influenced by a hug, which by a sad look.

A high pain tolerance to the point of denial characterizes these silent children. Dr. Yates noted "An eighteen-month-old boy was smiling doggedly through a difficult venipuncture. He put up not the slightest resistance." Their attitude seems to be similar to that of a small girl being adopted in my county. Beth's history showed she'd suffered many painful conditions without an external hint of what she was going through. When a nurse asked her why she didn't cry, the six year old solemnly looked her in the eye and said, "I go right over the pain."

Many private children such as Beth are never referred for treatment. In fact, probably the only reason they might would be if physical injuries were obvious. Although they may have endured severe emotional and possibly physical injuries for years, there seems at superficial glance to be little wrong with them. They adapt amazingly well to foster home settings, even multiple placements. Because they appear so placid, the devastating emptiness within may not be obvious except to therapists or rare individuals who see the real damage when revealed by stress.

This apparent absence of troublesome behaviors means only that the underlying anger stays bottled up in a "closed container." These children are time bombs waiting to explode, perhaps in adulthood, when certain events raise their stress to unmanageable levels.

Private children do not obey rules or authorities because they want to please or because they want to "be good." They are obedient because they don't want to be hurt. The concept of nurturing appears to be boring to them. They can move from one foster home to another with the greatest of ease, to many social workers' relief. The reason, however, should concern us.

From a psychoanalytic point of view, private children are dissimilar from the other types of abused children. The essential difference is that private children, unlike destructive or frightened ones, have received not only intensely negative, but also extremely positive, projections and feedback from abusing parents. Destructive and frightened children have no "identity crisis" as far as their parents see them: they are always bad, nasty or ungrateful. Private children, on the other hand, are often perceived by their parents as being especially beautiful, intelligent and so forth. They grow up with a highly grandiose sense of self, and tend to identify with the abusive (powerful) parent. Hospital staff noticed that when private children were visited by abusing parents, they would quickly but thoroughly "check out" parental moods or intention, then change their behavior accordingly. Their reactions depend on parental needs, not their own.

Developmental Delays

What accounts for the common finding of developmental delays among abused children? Many factors have been suggested. Abusive parents often show little patience with their children. They do not encourage imperfect attempts, but rather punish them.

The hypervigilance of maltreated children, as previously described, leaves little energy for exploring and learning. At home, one eye and ear must be watching and listening for threatening changes. These children are easily distracted in school and tend to be preoccupied by their fears and anxieties. Cognitive development is understandably delayed.

One study describes the trouble that neglected children have in pulling themselves together to deal with tasks. They were found to be easily distracted, low in impulse control, and inflexible in problem-solving. Compared to other types of abused children, the ones who had been seriously neglected without any physical abuse received the lowest ratings in self-esteem and were the most dependent.[8]

Psychological, as well as cognitive, development is often distorted. The need of the child to develop trust is thwarted when parents do not create a safe, warm and predictable world. Succeeding psychological tasks are then delayed or absent. Emotionally maltreated children come to believe they have little power to alter events, and they see life as "something that happens to you."

Self-control is generally not exhibited by an adult role model for these young victims. They see inconsistent adults who act aggressively, and sometimes violently, while punishing those same behaviors in the children. They have not seen people treat each other respectfully and with tolerance and good humor when differences of opinion occur. They identify with parents who have not learned to have friends or talk to each other without threats and unpleasantness.

Ronald and Evelyn Rohner's work on the effects of parental aggression and neglect suggests a number of personality and developmental dispositions not previously described. Their acceptance-rejection theory predicts—and cross-cultural tests have confirmed—that rejected children everywhere tend, more than accepted children, to be "dependent (clingy, intensely possessive) . . . because all humans have a basic need for positive response, but if a child's significant others are rejecting, his needs for warmth and affection are unfulfilled and he will, up to a point, increase his efforts to get love and attention. In other words, he will become dependent."[9]

That's to a certain point only. Then the dependency response may be extinguished or modified. The seriously neglected child has never learned to give love because he's never known a loving parent after whom his own behavior can be modeled. For various reasons, even though the rejected child craves love, he cannot accept it. This irony of the child most needing love and being the least able to love is one familiar to teachers, social workers and anyone who works with many children.

The Rohners discovered that though abused and neglected children may want to reach out to others, they are often unable to form satisfying relationships with others. As their already damaged sense of self-esteem is lowered further from unhappy relationships, they withdraw more and more into themselves. Another vicious circle.

When these children grow to adulthood, they tend to have overwhelming needs for affection which they cannot return because they have emotionally insulated themselves from personal relationships. These adults, if they become parents, are likely to reject their children for the same reason.

Freud is only one of many who has suggested that one of the most common ways of dealing with after-effects of a painful trauma is to arrange one's life in such a way that one "happens" to get into situations that repeat or re-enact the original event. The neglected child grown to be a parent makes the situation happen again in an effort to gain a sense of control over whatever it was that once was so hurtful and defeating. And so the circle of abuse and neglect continues.

Will it—can it—be broken?

Chapter Eight

The Mystery of Matthew

Resilient or "Invulnerable" Children

Matthew is a mystery. The son of unwed teenage parents, he was a severely neglected and scrawny baby who spent much of his early life in a succession of foster homes. By the time he was ten, his mother was in a perpetual alcoholic haze. No one had any idea where Matthew's father was. He had left Matt, a baby sister, and their mother without a trace five years earlier.

During her repeated chances to rehabilitate herself, Matthew's mother would pull herself together to get to her court hearings, resolved to lick her problems and care properly for her children. As her alcoholism grew progressively worse, she attempted to salvage some self-esteem and at the same time pay her bills by freelancing as a prostitute.

Matthew and his sister remember vividly the men who came around the house night and day. The sex they observed was raw and ugly, sometimes violent. Sometimes Matthew and his sister were molested. Mother didn't know or didn't care when the children stayed in their beds afterwards, crying and hoping to avoid further attention from her "friends."

Matthew's teachers compiled records that showed him to be neglected physically, emotionally, medically and educationally. He'd often be kept home from school to watch his sister when his mother went out to drum up business. He was encouraged by his mother to shoplift at grocery stores and was given lessons by her regarding how to react (tearfully) if caught.

In spite of all this and more, flying in the face of folk wisdom and scientific inquiry, Matthew is today at twenty-two graduating in the upper third of his college class with a double major in biology and chemistry. He has been a class officer, active in many extracurricular activities, and is extremely popular with teachers and peers. He is a thoughtful, caring young man who appears to have an enormous amount of quiet self-confidence. The future looks rosy for Matthew. But given his brutal and stressed childhood, how can his achievements and personality be explained?

Dr. E. James Anthony, one of the best-known researchers of resilient children, points out that one of the most significant inequalities of the future well-being of the individual is the inequality of risk. "For some, the world is secure, stable and predictable, they are born into acceptance, concern, and care; they are planned for, hoped for, and welcomed. For others the reverse is true. Life for them is short, sharp and brutish. They have parents who hate them from conception, reject them from birth, batter them as infants, neglect them as toddlers, and institutionalize or have them fostered at the drop of a hat. Nevertheless, two children from the same stock, the same womb, the same propitious or unpropitious environments may end up quite differently with one falling psychologically ill and the other apparently blossoming. A superchild may come out of the ghetto and a sad and sorry child from the well-to-do suburbs. Why and how? By what mysterious process of psychological selection is the one destroyed and the other preserved?"[1]

The mystery of Matthew—why and how some children manage to cope and even thrive despite appalling living conditions—is the mystery of what scientists have come to call resilient children. For them and others, the hope exists that if the puzzle of children like Matthew can be solved, other children might be helped to become similarly resilient.

In the past, resilient children have been pretty much ignored by professionals who concentrated on pathology rather than on protective factors. Most research has focused on what causes the problem, and little attention has been given to the factors that help individuals emerge healthy.

That tendency is beginning to change and, in the last decade, several researchers have begun investigating so-called "invulnerable" children. In Great Britain, Dr. Michael Rutter's work concentrates on the protective factors that help some children to triumph over the most severely deprived backgrounds. He focuses positively on the problem—factors that protect children—rather than the stresses they face. It is likely that research will proliferate on this subject, variously known as stress-resistance, ego-resilience, protective factors and invulnerability.

After years of observing "vulnerable" children, professionals began excitedly looking at "invulnerable" children, only to reject that word for a term less overstated. Even the most stress-resistant children are not free of the trauma they witnessed. One of the areas of research being investigated is the possible cost to the person's adult life from resiliency achieved in youth.

Dr. E. J. Anthony, professor of child psychiatry for eighteen years at St. Louis University, has studied the children of psychotic parents and found that certain children have an inordinate degree of resourcefulness and the ability to make something of very little. Scientists have yet to find a sure-fire combination of factors that produce a resilient child. Many have been identified, however, originating from various sources.

CONGENITAL TEMPERAMENT AND OTHER FACTORS

Resilient children tend to be born with "easy" temperaments. At birth, they are cuddly, easy to feed and care for and manage to win a great deal of positive attention from adult caretakers. Even though they may have mothers who are unresponsive, these children receive love and affection from others around them in a way less pleasant babies might not.

This easy-going temperament can protect the child in later life as well. Dr. Rutter discovered that "the temperamentally easy child tended to escape much of the flak" that their siblings might receive.[2]

One investigator found that the resilient child is more likely to have a robust physique, general good health and high energy levels,[3] another congenital factor.

Gender is apparently a factor as well. Dr. Rutter notes that in childhood, males are more vulnerable to both physical and emotional stress than are females. Girls, then, tend to be over-represented in the "superkid" category.[4] (According to several studies, females lose this coping advantage during adolescence.)

Family Characteristics

Even a child born with the sunniest of dispositions cannot survive—physically or emotionally—without *someone* looking out for her. Inevitably, studies of resilient children have uncovered at least one such person in their backgrounds. Perhaps it's one parent to whom the child relates well, or one who does a good job of parenting when not in jail, psychotic or drunk, or maybe it's a grandparent, aunt or other adult who goes out of his way for the child.

In the case of Barbara, a resilient child who lived with my family, the grandmother was the anchor and stability needed. The girl's mother, who was an alcoholic, often neglected her children badly and exhibited some bizarre actions during her sober periods. For Barbara, her grandmother was the person who demonstrated that life need not be chaotic and cruel. She obviously did a good job of modeling another lifestyle. Today Barbara is a college graduate, a lovely young wife and mother. Without her grandmother, she might not have been able to beat the odds.

The makeup of these children's families often includes people of varying age groups. Sometimes older brothers and sisters can serve as models. Often these siblings lived in the home before the environment came to be nearly intolerable. Somehow the children who show the most resilience have developed strong social bonds. Many of them were raised with religious faith and values transmitted by at least one family member.

While all children incorporate "good" and "bad" parts of their parents into their psychic makeup, children with abusive and neglectful parents don't have much of the "good" to work with. It appears to some researchers that resilient children use their imaginations more than other abused children. They incorporate the positive values they've seen in other parents, grandparents, family friends, teachers, social workers into their idea of their "good" parent. Somehow they put this jigsaw puzzle together into a mental picture of a "good" parent who is caring and loving.

For the children who are deprived of consistent love and care by the adults they depend on, this fantasy-substitute seems to help them cope. They are able to make sense of the world and to face life optimistically.

According to Dr. Anthony, parents of resilient children have been found to be less anxious than average parents, leaving more decisions to the child (sometimes severely taxing the child's maturity). These parents are less possessive and authoritarian, and are likely to allow the child "to do his own thing." If children do not cave in under this lack of protection and supervision, they tend to grow in confidence and resourcefulness "Confidence and competence go hand in hand," says Dr. Anthony.[5]

OTHER FACTORS

Resilient children tend to grow in social competence as they mature. They appear to be at ease with adults and other children. Unlike silent children (Chapter Seven), resilient children really do like adults and have a way of suggesting they have much to learn and would like to do so. It is an attitude that adults find winsome, and it's no wonder that such children are sometimes taken on as "protégés" by adults with whom they come in contact.

Adaptability

Stress-resistant children are flexible and creative in problem-solving. Somehow they have an ability to cope with changing circumstances and to "make the best of a bad situation." They are able to think of alternative solutions to problems more than other abused children.

Self-Confidence

Despite the stress in their lives, these children take pride in their ability to handle whatever life is dishing out. Rather than feeling sorry for themselves, they tend to view negative events as challenges to their competence. One child is described as making "bread sandwiches" so she would give the appearance of having lunch like her friends, even if the sandwiches had no filling. Throughout her life, "making a bread sandwich" became her metaphor whenever she had to cope with a problem. "I guess I'll just have to make a bread sandwich" meant she was able to competently meet another challenge.[6]

In a study conducted at the University of Minnesota, Dr. Norman Garmezy discovered resilient children have the ability to distance psychologically from mentally ill or disturbed parents, to defend against this kind of submissive, receptive involvement with psychotic parents that can lead to internalizing disturbed thought processes. He believes that the qualities of self-confidence, nonsubmissiveness and healthy skepticism are important for resilient children.[7]

Achievement

Probably the most influential factor other than temperament or family makeup is achievement. Resilient children are high achievers, tending toward extraordinary work in the arts. Although not unusually gifted intellectually, many are exceptionally original and creative. While the achieving experiences discovered did not tend to be academically oriented, they were often school-related. Success in sports, music, positions of leadership or special relationships with teachers were common. Sometimes the achievement was designation as the class clown or the repair of a piece of rundown equipment needed by the staff. Any success that gave children pleasure or a sense of being special was helpful.

For fortunate children who have known many successes, additional good experiences make little difference. The child who has come from a loving and nuturing home, has learned easily and enjoyed a feeling of importance, and his self-worth changes his view of himself and others little because he has had similar experiences in school. If, before attending school, however, a child has only had everything go against him, having good experiences in school (or in another setting) can make a tremendous difference.

These achievements seem to actually change children's views of themselves and of their ability to handle future problems. One of Dr. Rutter's conclusions is that neglected girls who had these good school experiences were more able to plan. This ability to plan has enabled previously neglected girls to find a harmonious relationship with a nondeviant man; and that relationship, which Rutter feels is a most protective factor for older girls, helps to develop resilience. The harmonious marriage was "so important it overwhelmed almost any other influence."

These girls were not just luckier than others in marrying good men. They had, however, planned their marriages. What this meant was that like many other institution-reared girls, they did not marry primarily to escape. Rather, these girls had known the men they married for six months or more, and then married for what were considered "positive" reasons.

Dr. Anthony proposes that a challenge/response formulation should be used to investigate some aspects of resilient children. One child faced with an overwhelming stress that threatens security may resort to "sick" behavior and perceive himself as a passive and helpless victim of fate. Magical thinking and fantasies of being rescued become life-long patterns. Another child, much less typical, responds to the same sort of stress by developing new behavior, behavior characterized by creativity, originality and resourcefulness that lift the child out and away from misery and craziness. Why does one child respond to the challenge with "sickness", the other with mastery?

Investigators such as Drs. Rutter, Garmezy and Anthony are researching questions such as these that will be of interest to all those who want to see the circle of abuse ended. Is the resilient child endowed with permanent "immunity", or does the constant need for mastery wear it down? At what price does resilience come? Are these children grown to adulthood able to form loving, trusting relationships, or do they retain throughout their later lives objectivity and detachment that helped them to survive?

Dr. Rutter's conclusions regarding the school's role in providing achievement opportunities for deprived children are important. He found that all schools were not equally effective in giving "second chances" to these children. The qualities which characterized the better schools included a setting of appropriately high expectations, good group management, effective feedback with ample use of praise, pleasant working conditions and conferral of trust and responsibility on pupils. Teachers in those schools modeled the type of competent, problem-solving behavior that children wanted to emulate.[8] The significance of the school's role—positively and negatively—related to the effects of emotional maltreatment are explained in the following chapter.

Chapter Nine

"Mostly I Just Want to Hide"

Emotional Maltreatment in the Schools

My daughter came home in tears from her elementary classroom one Friday and headed straight for her room. I followed her upstairs and found her sobbing on the bed. After some encouragement, she finally told me what had happened.

As one of their Weekly Reader exercises, the students were to put scrambled events in logical order. Katie had misunderstood a question early in the listing and consequently had ordered most of the letters wrong. A very conscientious student, she felt bad about this, but was unprepared for the shock of seeing her teacher red-pencil a huge F across the page, then hold it up for the attention of the class.

"Look, boys and girls," Mrs. White said. "Smarty-pants Katie got an F".

I wasn't there, of course, but I can imagine the mortification that must have flooded over my child. What lay behind the teacher's malice? Katie was—is—a straight A student whose performance is, if anything, too important to her.

Several of my friends who are teachers or administrators suggested I write a section on emotional abuse in the schools for this book. "It goes on a lot," one woman said. "Teachers and principals who wouldn't dare use corporal punishment on a student use humiliation, ridicule and other forms of verbal abuse with impugnity."

"Just don't leave any marks," one teacher reported was the guiding principle for discipline in her school. In these litigious days when people sue not only for legitimate but also for frivolous reasons, the treatment of the child is not the central issue, she said. Rather, it's avoiding anything that can be used in a court of law against the school. And as has been pointed out, the very nature of emotional abuse can be so subtle as to avoid recognition by many who would otherwise be concerned.

No meaningful statistics are available on the extent of the problem in the schools. But it does exist. Based on the information presented on the importance of positive school experiences in producing resilient children, one wonders how many already deprived and neglected children are made to feel even less self-esteem and competence because of what they experience at school.

Katie has recovered from her experience. She had good feelings about herself and her abilities before the teacher publicly shamed her. As far as I know, this incident was the only time she was treated in that manner by that teacher. Katie hadn't known a pattern of abuse, although in talking to other parents, I learned this particular teacher had been verbally abusive and shaming to many other students. One mother told me bitterly about the teacher's negative expectations for her son.

Randy had been placed in the far corner of the room at the beginning of the year. He soon figured out that Mrs. White was angry that he had been placed in her class after his previous placement in special education classes. The teacher expressed her resentment to other teachers at having a "low-achiever" in her room, and instead of doing what she could to encourage his potential, she berated his failures and overlooked his successes. This boy, who responded well to hugs, pats and other forms of physical reinforcement, met only with cold avoidance from Mrs. White. When he began crying in the mornings because it was time to go to school, Randy's parents finally demanded that he be moved to another classroom.

Mrs. White is still teaching. She is close to retirement and because of her husband's ill-health, many of her colleagues feel sorrier for her than for the children she has damaged. She has undoubtedly done at least an adequate job of teaching most average to high-achieving children. I wonder though how many children like Randy, who badly needed affirmation and encouragement from her, have instead received emotional abuse.

A Classroom Under Attack

Dr. Richard Krugman, a Denver pediatrician, observed twenty-seven children who were emotionally abused by their elementary teacher and found their behaviors to be noticeably different from previous years. The third and fourth graders in Mr. Clark's classroom began to undergo personality and behavior changes that were noticeable to their parents within the first two weeks of the beginning of the school year. None of these children reportedly had shown any of these troubling behaviors in previous years. When the symptoms listed first began showing up, most parents assumed they were caused by normal anxiety or having moved up a grade. As weeks went by, however, the symptoms did not disappear and parents began to become suspicious that the teacher's actions, rather than first-of-the-year jitters, were responsible for their children's distress.

The actions that students reported to their parents included "(1) verbal put-downs, harassment; (2) labeling ('stupid', 'dummy'); (3) inconsistent, erratic behavior; (4) screaming at children until they cried; (5) inappropriate threats to try to control the classroom; (6) allowing some children to harass and belittle others; (7) unrealistic academic goals for age/grade level; (8) use of homework as punishment; (9) fear-inducing techniques (e.g., tying a string to a child's chair and pulling it out from under him); (10) throwing homework at children and (11) physical punishments (punching, slapping, shaking and pulling ears)."[1]

Although Mr. Clark was pleasant to other adults, he turned into an abusive tyrant with students. The day after he had assigned several pages of homework, he tore up the students' work and threw it around, screaming at them and asking why they had done the assigned work.

What kind of symptoms resulted from this persistent emotional abuse? Dr. Krugman discovered that 88% of the teacher's students worried excessively about their performance, hearing comments such as "He'll kill me if I do it wrong," and perhaps more significantly, 76% of the students with previously positive self-concepts developed negative self-perceptions, believing "I'm dumb, I can't do it." The same percentage of change occurred in students who had previously liked school and came to hate it while Mr. Clark was their teacher. Nearly as many were afraid the teacher would hurt them. Psychosomatic illnesses such as headaches and stomachaches were common, and other symptoms such as nightmares and sleep disturbances, withdrawal and refusal to go to school were observed.

When some parents had their children removed from Mr. Clark's classroom, their children's symptoms disappeared. This established a clear relationship betwen symptoms and the teacher's behavior, and other parents requested that their youngsters, too, be moved.

Unfortunately, the school administration did not respond positively at this point. They took the position that Mr. Clark's teaching was not the issue, but rather, "overprotective parents who had been taken in by their attention-seeking children." In fact, school administrators tried to assure some parents that "your family is the only one to complain."

Many parents and teachers report that noninvolvement in correcting the problem is a common situation. The abusive behaviors are often denied or at most minimally addressed. In effect, the administration thereby perpetuates the abuse. In Katie's case, the administration took the position that Mrs. White was so worried about her husband's health that she really shouldn't be held responsible for her outbursts.

Some educators defend emotional abuse (humiliation, screaming, name-calling), maintaining that it "toughens" a child. Such a view is totally insupportable by the evidence which tells us that self-esteem and personal strength are built from positive, rather than negative, self-perception.

In the annual Gallup poll of the public's attitudes toward public schools, respondents consistently ranked discipline as the major problem plaguing U.S. education. Many teachers appear to share this view. Perhaps this perception accounts for some of the "get tough" attitude that includes a degree of willingness to accept children's emotional injury by school personnel as a valid form of discipline. It stands to reason that if a teacher is not discouraged from abusing a child like Katie, who has always been a docile and willing student, that teacher will likely use abusive discipline methods with less compliant pupils.

If we look at the causes of disciplinary problems in the school, the reasons why emotionally abusive treatment is not only cruel, but ineffective as well, become more obvious. Some of these causes include (1) inadequate parenting of students; (2) ineffective teacher training; (3) congenital temperament (children who are easily distracted or unable to persevere); (4) lack of consistency in disciplinary actions; (5) inappropriate placement of and/or expectations for students; (6) frustration because of learning problems; (7) poor self-esteem; (8) overexposure to violence as a way of problem-solving; (9) peer pressure; (10) a history of child abuse that in turn "invites" abuse by others.

Professionals within the school have suggested that the classrooms which are characterized by extreme quiet may not be the havens of learning they appear to be. In the case of Mr. Clark, his principal interpreted the quiet, which was really due to children's attempts not to antagonize the teacher further, as being a sign of Mr. Clark's good classroom control. Dr. Krugman states, "The children's reactions to Mr. Clark's behavior parallel observations made of children with abusive parents; these children often seem overanxious to please the parent despite repeated rejection." [2]

Myths abound about the values of verbal punishment. One of these myths is the belief that public shaming builds character. Research simply does not support this activity in the schools any more than it supports it in the home. A person's conscience is not developed by being ridiculed. Instead, praise and warmth have been found to foster moral development.

A second belief about emotionally coercive behavior is that it teaches respect. If respect is the same as anxiety and avoidance, then that belief is indeed true. But if respect is the esteem in which we hold others, berating and labeling will not be effective. In fact, it often causes the victim and witnesses to lose respect for the abusive person.

A third myth about punishment is that it is the only way to get through to some students, typically, poor, minority-group males. If they have known only abusive discipline at home, these children may appear to invite further abuse from teachers and administrators who feel justified in using these methods in particular on all poor, minority-group males.

Alternatives to the educationally unsound practice of using emotionally and/or physically abusive methods need to be explored. It is important that the child who has not learned positive discipline at home learn it in the schools. As one teacher ruefully said, "While it's not true that punishment is the only thing that some children understand, it is true that it's the only form of discipline some *teachers* understand."

One educator primarily blames inadequate teacher preparation for student abuse. "Such teachers," she writes, "may have difficulty in communication, lack self-esteem or exhibit immaturity in relationships with others. Personal and training inadequacies make it impossible for many teachers to recognize their contribution to a child's behavior, or even perceive the problems of a child under stress. A child is subject to institutional abuse if he is compelled to work with a teacher not of his choice, in a school condoning violence, failing to motivate him or not seeking reasons for his lack of success.

"Teachers who give demeaning punishment, 'speak down,' always disbelieve, make a child appear a fool, use a child as a butt for caustic wit or sadistic treatment, assume a child is always bad, make constant demands for "even better" performance, should not be in contact with a growing child. A caustic or mildly sadistic teacher, insensitive, unable or not attempting to understand the developmental stage at which a child has arrived, using methods that she considers perfectly legitimate to maintain discipline . . . makes a positive contribution to the alienation of the child."[3]

Potential School Problems

Some of the potential results of emotional punishment inflicted by school personnel have been described. Several others are reported by parents and teachers.

Broken communication between teacher and student generally results from emotional punishment. Seldom can positive communication happen between a punished student and punitive teacher, at least for some time following the incident. This means lost learning time for the student whose frame of mind will undoubtedly not be conducive to learning. Besides the student's time lost to subject material, the teacher has wasted an opportunity to demonstrate that problems can be handled calmly and without hostility.

Loss of self-esteem. The child who experiences ridicule, low expectations and the like will find it difficult to develop or keep a sense of self-esteem. Through a pattern of emotionally abusive punishment, self-esteem can be systematically destroyed, as happend to children in Mr. Clark's classroom. Unfortunately, this loss of self-esteem often occurs among the children who have the most to lose because they are also receiving negative messages in their homes. This is all the more unfortunate since many apparently defeated children manage to regain control of their lives and a high degree of self-esteem only as a result of rewarding experiences in school. Such was the case for a large number of children described by Dr. Michael Rutter's study of resilient children.[4]

Anti-social behavior. Sometimes emotional abuse in schools produces avoidant, anxious behavior that is noticed primarily by parents. Younger children tend to "shut down" and seem depressed. Children with aggressive temperaments may retaliate with vandalism against the school or teachers' property, or act violently toward teachers, students or perhaps pets and brothers and sisters.

Another set of behaviors commonly found among children emotionally abused by the schools demonstrates the mechanism of protective defense. Children "save" their strength by attempting to function all day at school in a way that avoids further abuse; they "let down" in a safe place in the evenings.[5] Dr. Krugman describes "what on the surface to outsiders seemed to be a functioning schoolchild during the day because he was 'well-behaved', was, in reality, a child under attack, who at home would cry or scream during sleep or refuse to go to scout meetings or participate in sports and generally disclosed the extent of anxiety in his own individual manner."

Lowered expectations. Verbal and emotional abuse have been shown to result in lowered expectations. On the other hand, the positive expectations of the teachers led to higher IQ scores in children, especially on verbal and information subtests. This so-called "Pygmalion effect" has demonstrated in dozens of studies that the experimenter's or teacher's expectations made a significant difference in students' measured performance.

Robert Rosenthal explains the influence of the Pygmalion effect as follows: People who have been led to expect good things from their students (or children, or clients) appear to

1. create a warmer social–emotional climate around their "special students";
2. give more feedback to these students regarding their performance;
3. teach more material, and more difficult material, to these students;
4. give them more opportunities to respond and question.

He also concluded that when a child who is not expected to do well does so, his teacher often actually looks upon that behavior and personality as undesirable. This finding was especially true in low-ability classrooms. Teachers who may have a difficult time believing that a "low-ability" labeled child can have an intellectual spurt can interpret the change as "troublemaking." They may feel the child "doesn't know his place." Since similar results occurred in several studies, the initial study cannot be dismissed as a fluke.[6]

While appropriate punishment need not be banished from the classroom, it should not be relied upon as *the* way to change behavior. One teacher suggests that there is nothing wrong with punishing a child *if* the punishment fits the crime and *if* the teacher doesn't get upset and out of control when punishing the student.

Inviting Success

Another teacher believes that instead of depending on punishment, educators "invite success" from students. This notion that students behave in accordance with a teacher's perception of them can be used for good or bad. To use it in a positive sense means the teacher will continuously be transmitting to the students the message that they are responsible, capable, and valuable. This principle can be the foundation on which the teacher's entire philosophy is grounded. It will find countless opportunities to say to students, "I care about you. I trust you. I know you can learn. I am here to help you."

While the principle of inviting success rightly expresses itself in positive terms, teachers using it must examine words and actions that might be contradictory. Sarcasm, ridicule, and frequent use of words such as "stop", "no", and "can't" work at cross-purposes to perceiving children as trustworthy and capable.

Some time ago, I had the pleasure of observing an elementary classroom where the teacher, a perky young woman, based her methods on the invitation-to-success principle. Although she had well over twenty children of varying ability levels in her classroom, the atmosphere was one of contented busyness. She maintained excellent eye contact with her pupils, frequently used their names and by smiles and brief touch, constantly encouraged high-, middle- or low achieving students to do their best. She was able to achieve a degree of cooperation among the group that appeared to minimize the number of children who saw themselves as "losers."

She explained to me that while she approves of the "striving for excellence" movement currently in vogue, she fears it may lessen the already low self-esteem and motivation of noncompetitive and low-ability pupils. To achieve a balance, she works to develop activities that can require cooperation, instead of competition, and rewards nonintellectual efforts, as well as academic ones. She uses praise in creative ways including congratulatory letters or phone calls to parents of her students, arranges for educational games and learning centers and encourages children to cooperate in ways that utilize unique abilities often overlooked by parents or other teachers. Often she tries to include parents as guest speakers or "entertainment leaders" and has discovered this can improve parent-child respect and appreciation.

Her students seemed extraordinarily sensitive to the teacher's expectations, and she to their varying needs. Like many teachers whom researchers have found anticipate superior performance, she possessed a self-assurance that seemed to flow out to her pupils.

Undoubtedly, as the topic of emotional maltreatment becomes more operationally definable, its presence in the classroom will be increasingly reported. I would hope that in the future, teacher training and personnel policies will address the problem. For some children, an emotionally healing classroom is their best chance for a happy and productive future. The teachers and administrators who work toward this goal deserve commendation by the public.

The sad remark by one boy in Mr. Clark's Denver classroom—"Mostly I just wanted to hide"—should not be the sentiment of any student.

Chapter Ten

We All Need a Little Help
from Our Friends

The Prevention and Treatment of Child Abuse

During the months I spent writing this book, many harrowing incidents of emotional maltreatment of children came to my attention, some of them involving children with whom I directly work. A few of their stories have found their way into print, but most will never be known in their desolate and dreary detail except to a few professionals and the children themselves. The families involved are of all kinds: very poor to upper middle-class; blue-collar to executive; married and single parents. The externals don't appear to matter much. The common denominator is parents who willfully or unknowingly destroy their children's spirits.

Vignettes, case studies and attempts at a definitive explanation of emotional maltreatment can only be helpful to a point. Condemning a parent for rejecting her baby, then pushing the whole sordid matter aside is easier than accepting the truth of a societal problem. Our moral outrage at such parents isolates even more those who wound their children, and adds to the distress that brings them to that point. Then comes the time that prevention and treatment are appropriate topics, unless the question is being approached from a purely academic viewpoint. For someone like myself who daily sees the living results of maltreatment, the need for appropriate strategies goes beyond formulating theories. Ways to treat, or more importantly, prevent, the cyclical effects of child abuse in practical, efficient and cost-effective ways are urgently needed. Again, as with the problem of defining emotional maltreatment, considerable dispute exists among parties involved as to what treatment or prevention methods are effective.

Thinking about courses of action reminded me of an incident of a few years ago. At that time my family was living in a new, upper middle-class neighborhood. Most of the homes had been built within the previous year or so, and with few exceptions, the families had two employed parents. An annual block party provided the only opportunity for many people to talk with their neighbors. Support and communication among the families on the block was virtually nil; it was not uncommon for people to be unaware of their neighbors' names. When a problem developed affecting several of the families, people were uncertain as to how it should be handled.

A sixth grader, Jeff Buchanan, whose parents owned a lovely home in the neighborhood, had been terrorizing younger children by lying in wait for them as they returned home from school. When one or two came along he teased, menaced, and attacked them, leaving no serious physical injuries but plenty of fear and anger on the part of his victims.

As more children were caught and bullied by the boy, parents' consternation spread about what to do. One mother confided to another that by herself she had tracked down Jeff one afternoon and threatened him with "real trouble" if he ever laid a hand on her child again. The boy looked at her, unimpressed, and said coldly that he'd kill her if she did anything. When the mother related this to a neighbor, she found that the boy came from an abusive situation. "If you tell his parents, I know they'll be even more brutal to him," the neighbor said.

A call to the school for information didn't help. Because of confidentiality laws, the principal was unable to say much. It was obvious that the boy was well-known for discipline problems. The principal didn't have many ideas, but implied that the boy's parents were largely to blame.

Rumors and suggestions floated around the neighborhood and for once gave neighbors—at least those with small children—some common concern. The inadequacies of the parents, their relative isolation, their lack of supervision of their child, all were discussed. What was remarkable about the whole situation was that no one seemed able to come up with a solution.

A father said he was calling the police, but someone else demurred, reminding him that seldom did the troublemaker actually physically assault a child. Someone else suggested calling child welfare and asking them to investigate. This idea too was dropped. No one wanted to make the parents angrier than they usually appeared to be toward their son.

How about a person in the neighborhood talking in a low-key manner to the parents? Maybe they didn't "know better" and just needed to take a parenting course, someone offered. Not one person in the neighborhood had a relationship with either parent that would provide an opportunity for such a visit.

That episode with the Buchanan family is significant, I think, for several reasons. When it became known that the abusive boy had abusing parents, no unanimity could be found as to what course of action to take. Punitive? Helpful? The same sort of disagreement is found among professionals.

And instead of looking at some of the larger problems, such as the isolation and lack of support within the neighborhood, at least initially, the parents on the block concentrated on the "pathology" of the individual boy and his family.

Ecological Perspective

This is a typical attitude. We tend to think of child abuse and neglect— as we do most problems—as the result of individual deficiency or pathology. We concentrate on parents who are alcoholic, mentally ill or hold unrealistic expectations about what children can and should not do. As a result of this orientation, individuals' or couples' rehabilitation is sought.

While unquestionably this perspective has some merit, we can't wait for society to be changed before we help children who are desperately hurting right now; it oversimplifies the problem. Abuse and neglect are not only problems of individual children and their parents, but also issues of the larger society. Dr. Karl Menninger once said, "What's done to children, they will do to society."[1] The opposite of that is also true.

One of the more exciting and useful recent developments in the psychosocial field is the growing awareness that we cannot understand human behavior apart from the social situation in which it occurs. Common sense and life experience tell us that people's actions are profoundly affected by who and what is happening around them, and countless research projects prove it. One of the findings that has been publicized in the popular press, for example, shows that people who witness emergencies in conjunction with other bystanders are less likely to give aid than those who witness an emergency alone.

While not minimizing the individual's characteristics, these findings underline the importance of looking at an issue such as child abuse as *interaction* between individuals and their environment. Developmental psychologist Urie Bronfenbrenner is one of the leaders of this "ecological" approach to parent-child relationships. It emphasizes the significance of "quality of life" for families and the value of socially supportive environments in creating that life. According to Bronfenbrenner, parents do better when they receive plenty of nurturing themselves from formal and informal relationships. Childrearing is a challenge, and parents who have easy access to guidance and support, whether from friends, neighbors, or professionals, generally feel better about themselves and their children. Because a rich social environment has this effect, Bronfenbrenner believes proposed changes must focus not on "who cares for the children, but who cares for those who care."[2] The nurturers need nurturing, he asserts.

The need for this support is not limited to the poor. Although affluence allows the luxury of purchasing services and activities unavailable to those living in poverty, loneliness and alienation know no class boundaries. Because of high mobility, lack of extended family contacts and other reasons, upper middle-class families require enduring connections and assistance as much as others who are less financially well-off.

Our insistence on "rugged individualism" is considered by many to explain America's relatively high rate of child abuse. Americans have a long history of "going it alone." Alexis de Tocqueville pointed out in his nineteenth-century *Democracy in America:* "Individualism (in America) is considered a tranquil sentiment which leads each citizen to isolate himself from the mass of his fellows and retire, aloof, with his family and friends."

More recently, David Riesman and Philip Slater, authors of *The Lonely Crowd* and *The Pursuit of Loneliness* respectively, commented on the increasing alienation, disconnection and boredom of the American people because of the emphasis on individualism.

In a five-year study just released, Robert Bellah describes the lives of 250 educated, middle-class Americans. *Habits of the Heart* is a fascinating look at a small group of people whose relationships and attitudes are typical of the larger society. According to Bellah, in contrast to the past, relationships today are continually evaluated for personal gains and losses, then renegotiated when considered to be in the individual's best interest. His observations seem to be in line with case histories presented in this book. For some, not only relationships with spouses, but those with children as well are considered negotiable as these lone individuals pursue meaning without commitment and happiness without permanence.[3]

While a history of emotional deprivation in one's own childhood, low self-esteem and other factors previously mentioned put individuals in a "high risk" category for child maltreatment, the ecological approach contends that it is the *social context* in which families live that changes risk to actual abuse. Repeatedly, social isolation has been shown as a correlate of child maltreatment. This is not to say that the isolation causes abuse, but rather that it is an indicator of possible trouble. Often the people who live in social isolation have a lifelong pattern of estrangement. Broken relationships with family, friends and marriage partners are common. These are people who cannot sustain relationships that require any level of commitment. By their behavior and attitudes, they drive away others who would be friendly and supportive.

Most attempts to improve the lot of neglected and abused children focus on parents, seeking to improve their parenting skills, understanding of child development and so forth. I wish I could believe these attempts are usually successful. Many, if not most, neglectful parents are highly resistive to change. Abusive parents who are not also neglectful parents present somewhat less of a challenge, but nevertheless, these persons are hard to reach. Large numbers try to escape their pain through drugs, alcohol or by sleeping most of the day. Chronic depression, borderline mental functioning and other forms of emotional problems are common.

Change, if it comes, comes slowly. A mother may finally be impressed with the necessity to talk to her children, but then forgets about providing food. While some parents are trying, they may change too slowly to prevent significant and permanent damage to a child's body, mind, and spirit.

People Who Can't Parent

Another issue in prevention and treatment requires honestly facing up to the fact that not all people can or want to be adequate parents. The abusive circle cannot be broken as long as people believe everyone is "naturally" or "instinctively" suited for parenthood. My hope is that the information presented to this point indicates faulty attachment between parent and child, whatever its cause, is not a problem easily remedied.

"I can't imagine a parent not loving her children. It's just not natural" is a comment heard frequently by child protection workers. That remark reflects society's view that parental rejection is unnatural, and that such rejection will disappear if parents can be "taught" and destructive influences, such as alcoholism or poverty, are eliminated. My experience and that of many others shows this to be untrue.

Many of the coldest, most rejecting parents with whom I've worked have had all the knowledge and resources that could be reasonably provided. Many of them are intelligent, affluent, "beautiful" people. Yet they are not parent material.

Why? As a result of their backgrounds (attachment disorders, psychological inadequacies, or other reasons) these people cannot be loving parents. They seem to have no more capacity or desire for nurturing than a turtle that lays its eggs before moving on. Like Harlow's deprived monkey mothers, if not physically violent to their offspring, they are emotionally rejecting and unable to form normal attachments.

If we are serious about breaking the circle of emotional maltreatment, we cannot continue to assume that every person can attach to children. The persons least able to parent are those who have the fewest personal resources to bring to their children, but ironically, they also expect the most rewards from their children. Such parents expect their children to make up for everything missing in their own worlds.

Dr. R. E. Helfer writes in *Childhood Comes First: A Crash Course in Childhood for Parents* that many parents who themselves grew up with an inadequate parent-child relationship have never developed the capacity to relate touch to pleasurable sensation. These are parents who have no desire to cuddle, stroke, rub, kiss and snuggle their child even in infancy. No amount of parenting education seems to change such parents who are only threatened by physical touch or who associate it with violence.[4] This lack of desire for physical touch with the infant can, and should be, one of the early warning signs that the attachment needs of the child probably won't be met. The most difficult, if not impossible, parent to change is the one who has a good intellectual understanding of the child, but who chooses not to deal with her because of his own too-great personal needs, the parents who vainly seeks self-satisfaction in compensation for his own early attachment failure.

This does not imply that inadequate parenting skills and knowledge cannot contribute greatly to a maltreatment situation. When such ignorance is compounded with other stresses, such as poverty and lack of support, of course, the risk for neglect or abuse rises. The biggest challenge to treatment and prevention is when these inadequacies are compounded by personal emotional failings. Many of the mothers described in Haynes' study of failure-to-thrive babies fall into this category. Those women who deliberately withheld food from their babies, or pinched and otherwise hurt them, reveal the dangerous nature of insufficient skills and knowledge overlaid with a personal inability to love and nurture.

For such parents, merely learning a skill does not guarantee its use. If the parent is hurting from his early lack of attachment, "knowing the steps" does not ensure more effective nurturing of children. Nevertheless, some experts believe that more positive behavior, even if unmotivated by nobly altruistic parental feelings, can help those children to become better parents themselves someday.

Many maltreating parents—even intelligent ones—who are exposed to parenting and child development classes have no idea what is meant by abstractions such as "treating children like persons." A parent who can only perceive the child as someone who should be controlled, or who partakes of scarce resources, or who holds specific requirements for the child based on personal needs, has no way of conceptualizing how to treat a child with respect and dignity.

I'm currently involved in the placement of a seriously disturbed fifteen year old. Nate's natural mother is an advertising executive in a distant city. By her own report, she sought therapy for herself when Nate was three because she was unable to hold or touch him without revulsion. Extreme coldness and mechanical caregiving, as well as his parents' divorce when he was six, are all Nate remembers of his early years. When Nate was about nine, he began fondling his six-year-old sister. This situation intensified and continued for three years until it was discovered by Nate's father and stepmother.

I doubt if any parenting classes could break through to this cold, elegant businesswoman who now, even more, rejects her son. In no way does she appear to connect her icy detachment toward her boy with his later twisted attempts to find warmth and acceptance from his sister. Unless she learns through therapy how to deal with the source of her rejecting behavior—and at present she doesn't believe she has any problems—all the facts or humane approaches to successful parenting will be in vain.

With these reservations in mind, coupled with a scarcity of dollars and therapists to deal with abusive prevention and treatment, it is easy to see why the struggle against the maltreatment of children seems to be a losing battle. On a personal level, I perceive and feel a degree of burnout among my colleagues "in the trenches" who get discouraged from the intensity and stubbornness of the problem. When a worker has labored for months to improve a family situation, only to learn that the child again has been severely abused or neglected, the sense of defeat can become unbearable.

The Need for Prevention

While I was interviewing various professionals, one major source of frustration was overwhelmingly mentioned. That was the fact that services are so seldom preventative; instead, services cannot be provided until the family situation has deteriorated almost to the point of no return. Instead of putting our dollars and time into "habilitation," we try to "rehabilitate" families. As many experts have shown, the recidivism rate among abusive or neglectful parents is ample evidence that our current approach is inadequate.

Studies have shown that a course of action more effective than treating hard-core neglecting and abusing parents is identifying and working with children before patterns have become firmly established. The earlier such intervention occurs, the greater the likelihood that children will not suffer profoundly from the effects of neglect or abuse. A dual focus on improving the condition of both parents and children seems to be the ideal treatment.

In the struggle against child maltreatment, several hard questions remain to be answered. First, if Americans are serious about breaking the circle of abuse, prevention rather than treatment must become the priority. *Are we willing to see tax dollars, as well as the private economy, focus on methods of prevention?* Instead of paying out billions for foster care, aid to families with dependent children, drug and alcohol-related crime and suffering, prison and other institutional costs in reaction to the problems, Americans can choose to concentrate on preventing the problems by seeking ways to strengthen the family. We need to find answers: *How can the pathology of particular environments be eradicated? How can we encourage the kinds of environments that enrich and support parent-child relationships? How can we help hurting families receive help in a manner that does not rob them of dignity?*

Few would deny that preventative programs stressing mutual helpfulness, support and concern are vastly preferable to service intervention. Court-ordered parenting classes are not nearly so likely to be effective as noncoercive, nonintrusive help from friends and neighbors. While the formal system is certainly required for a variety of reasons, personal social networks can be far more important in strengthening families and preventing the social isolation and loneliness that encourages child maltreatment.

I reject the notion set forth by some sociologists that America needs a national family policy. Because of the cultural and ethnic diversity of our backgrounds, no meaningful policy could be established that would not be offensive to some people. Nevertheless, some national commitment to strengthening families seems to be warranted. Americans have traditionally sought to keep government policy, as much as possible, at the local level. By building on virtues such as freedom, neighborliness, and helpfulness, we can minimize bureaucratic distance and unconcern.

Neighborhood and community prevention strategies can be directed toward reducing stress factors and increasing resources, such as coping and nurturing skills and support groups. The specific ways these strategies are implemented may vary from one community to another. In my own, some of the ways these changes are being made, include reducing birth defects through an emphasis on prenatal nutrition and care. For those low-income women who qualify, wholesome, "non-junk" foodstuffs are provided, along with guidelines for preparation. The program is inadequate in many ways, but it's a start.

Around the country people are creating options and resources for today's parents. Instead of heavy reliance on institutions or professionals, we must look to parents to become committed to providing support for each other.

They see mutual support as a key factor in increasing parental satisfaction and effectiveness.

One such informal group, PEP (Postpartum Education for Parents) was begun by Jane Honikman several years ago in Santa Barbara, California. After the birth of her first baby, Jane's isolation, uncertainty and loneliness drove her to sharing her feelings with other parents whom she discovered felt the same way. Out of their conversations came a group for parents in which to share information and experiences. They started a "warm line", an answering service staffed by volunteers on a 24-hour basis. The warm-line staff use their own experiences as a resource to answer questions and offer support. Sometimes they refer callers to specialists or parents who have hade rather unique experiences that might be helpful. Jane Honikman credits the success of her group and others like it to the fact that parents need and appreciate the knowledge that they are not alone.

Another group, also begun in California, was given the unlikely name of Bananas by its three originators who thought they were "going bananas" from staying home with their babies without any breaks. They began simply by forming a communications network with other parents who wished to start co-op play groups to give themselves some free time away from their toddlers. It grew to an organization large enough to help find excellent day care for children anywhere in the U.S. Its newsletter advocates various family concerns and encourages legislation that strengthens and supports the family in various communities.

Dealing with stress and exploitation can be more difficult. In my community, support groups and assertiveness training for women provide understanding for people coping with problems ranging from alcoholism and drug abuse to the battered-woman syndrome. Programs, such as those offered by Big Brothers/Big Sisters, Boys' and Girls' Clubs and the YWCA, build self-esteem and competence among children, as well as stressed parents. Research is very clear that people involved in self-help and/or support groups are much better off emotionally than their counterparts who attempt to face their problems alone. A study of the impact of Parents' Anonymous groups (a support group for abusive parents seeking to change their behavior) shows that this group is generally more effective than formal, intrusive services.[5]

Many abusive parents, though, as pointed out, do not perceive themselves as having a problem, and certainly have no intention of joining a support group to improve their parenting skills. None of the parents I described in the beginning of this chapter seemed open to support from their neighbors, let alone from strangers. What sort of approach should be taken with such parents?

Few professionals from the various disciplines which fight the battle against child abuse deny that adults must be held accountable for intentional actions that damage children's development. This underlines the responsibility of health, educational and other community resources to ensure that the lower limits of acceptable child care are most clearly understood by anyone caring for children. If this responsibility is not met, society is an accessory to abuse and neglect.

While nurturing parents may be offended by the "lower limit" criterion, it is often the approach used in law and in practice. Without these lower limits within the community, we have no criteria for taking action. It is in this area, Garbarino states, that child development experts need to push for an understanding of an operational definition as to what constitutes threats to a child's competence.[6]

In dealing with this thorny problem, one should note the desirability of teaching children in early childhood both the motives for and skills in affiliating and helping. In early childhood we can more easily lay the foundations for caring and helping relationships. Such skills as cooperating, listening attentively, disagreeing in a way that does not rob anyone of respect, while ideally taught from toddlerhood in the home, can be reinforced by the schools.

What can be done right now to reach punitive, abusive parents? The concept of "community gatekeepers" gives some clues. Evidence suggests that people whose work brings them into regular contact with the public are often trusted and are in a position to provide support to others. Members of religious, legal, educational and health institutions are often in a good position to observe and, to some degree, deal with the stress of those whom they serve in other capacities.

Even more effective, for many people who feel intimidated by the demeanor or credentials of a pastor or doctor, are neighborhood figures such as bartenders, beauticians, merchants or clerks and the like. The image of the attentive bartender-psychiatrist is a familiar one; and most women can relate to either having heard impressive problems told to hairdressers, or perhaps to confiding themselves in such an "informal" helper.

Community gatekeepers and informal helpers seem to provide the best avenue for reaching people like the Buchanans. All but the most pathological families seek medical attention, buy groceries and clothing, get their hair cut professionally, and in other ways venture out of their homes. I believe professionals tend to overlook the potential of such opportunities for breaking through the isolation and privacy of the "hard-to-reach" maltreating parents, but such helpers themselves may need greater understanding and more skills in reaching out to hard-to-know people.

Benjamin H. Gottlieb describes an innovative outreach program designed to link families to new community attachments. "Our program . . . is being conducted in collaboration with three local family physicians. These physicians are convening parent support groups composed of eight to ten couples drawn from each of their practices. The couples are randomly selected, instead of being chosen on the basis of their vulnerability. Since the emphasis is on primary prevention, there is no stigma associated with participation . . .

"Although the physicians will offer medical information when appropriate and will distribute some educational material about child development, nutrition and parent-child interaction, the focus is on the parents' own needs. We want to create a situation in which people can comfortably share experiences and as the process of social comparison unfolds, can obtain both direct and indirect feedback about their own norms, behavior and feelings as parents. We hope to expand the participants' repertoires of problem-solving behaviors that can be used when stressful family situations arise . . . we have even toyed with the idea of setting up a "buddy system." [7]

Gottlieb concedes that families overburdened by the demands of everyday life do not have the time or energy to cultivate relationships that support families, and he admits that, for many parents, slumping in front of the television is the easiest way to fill whatever leisure time exists. Such parents, seeing their children's demands and needs as burdens, resist any additional involvements. Whether parents retreat or become overinvolved in community affairs, it is at the expense of their children; and the family must reconsider its priorities.

"Just as we now think it is appropriate to borrow a cup of sugar, we can invent ways to make it possible for people to borrow help in handling life's routine ups and downs," Gottlieb concludes. We all need a little help from our friends. By utilizing informal helpers and gatekeepers who are sensitive to the emotional needs of those with whom they come in contact, and by developing neighborhood support groups, many of the problems leading to child maltreatment can be prevented. Would-be-helpful neighbors need to be given more assistance in knowing where and how to intervene if they strongly suspect child abuse. Learning how not to "barge in", but rather support and encourage natural neighbors in coming to their own conclusions, is an art and skill which could be taught in every community.

Ellen Gray and Joan DiLeonardi have written an excellent pamphlet that helps professional and lay helpers in evaluating child abuse prevention programs. In their foreward, they stress that "Child abuse is a community problem, and its prevention is a community responsibility. The community must provide parents and children with certain supports, training and information to help them cope successfully with their roles in the family.

" . . . . While the experts seemed to agree that the earlier support can be provided the better, they acknowledged that for child abuse to be prevented, families need support at many different times. Thus, they identified programs directed toward each phase of the life cycle, beginning with the prenatal period and continuing through the school years. These programs include:

1. Perinatal support programs—to prepare individuals for the job of parenting and to enhance parent-child bonding.

2. Education for parents—to provide parents with information about child development and with skills in child care.

3. Early and periodic childhood screening and treatment—to identify and deal with physical and developmental problems in children at an early age.

4. Programs for abused children—to minimize the longer term effects on children who have been abused and to reduce the likelihood of their becoming abusive parents.

5. Social skills training for children and young adults—to equip young people with skills and knowledge necessary to succeed in adulthood.

6. Mutual aid programs and neighborhood support groups—to reduce the social isolation so often associated with abuse.

7. Family support services, including health care, family planning, child care, crisis care (such as hot-line counseling) marriage counseling and

related services—to provide families with the range of supports they need to survive the stresses of life and to stay together.

8. Public information on child abuse—to heighten the public's awareness about different types of abuse and neglect and to provide specific information on how abuse can be prevented and where the parents can turn for help."[8]

These programs will not come easily or cheaply, although cost-effectiveness could be shown for those less interested in human misery than in dollars.

While They're Young: Good News/Bad News

The good news is that one encouraging sign for the future is seen in the increasing number of boys, as well as girls, who are taking child development and family living courses while in high school. The bad news is that at the same time, the number of teen pregnancies is increasing. If the trend continues, within the decade four out of ten girls will become pregnant in their teens. This trend is alarming since teenage parenthood is often associated with health problems for both mother and child, poor educational attainment and employment prospects, isolation and other precursors of child maltreatment. In reaction, the federal government has instituted a new program known as the Adolescent Family Life Program, but nicknamed "Project Chastity." In contrast to most such programs that emphasize contraception, Project Chastity encourages sexual abstinence, a rather surprising change in this permissive era. So far over 15,000 teens have been reached by the program that began in 1982.

Those teenagers who are already pregnant or have delivered are not ignored. For them, a wide range of health, education and social services are provided, and adoption is actively promoted as an alternative to abortion. In fact, abortion specifically cannot be encouraged or permitted under the program, a feature that has raised the ire of some pro-abortion factions.

Preliminary research at Utah State University indicates that an experimental student group who participated in a "Project Chastity" curriculum showed less permissive attitudes toward premarital sex, more communication with their parents about sexual and other matters, and a generally more informed and positive view of family life. It would appear that many of the features of "Project Chastity" could be incorporated on a local level by schools and other programs.

The Need for Intervention

One of the complex questions about which much disagreement exists is *When is intervention appropriate?* Bitter and highly emotional differences of opinion exist among families and professionals as to when, if ever, the state has the right to intervene. *(See Tables 2 & 3, pp. 136–138.)*

In my own community, passions rose so high among parents whose children were removed for abuse and neglect that bomb threats were made against people working in the social services building. Less volatile parents ask, "What right does the government have to meddle in people's lives? What right do judges, attorneys and social workers have to prescribe how and under what conditions children can be punished?" The questions regarding the right to family privacy versus the rights of children to be protected and adequately cared for have led to violent differences of opinion in the past and will, undoubtedly, do so in the future.

In many communities the religious right has teamed up with disgruntled parents who sincerely seem to believe that any form of discipline is warranted, even physical violence directed at toddlers and older children that produce scars and bruises. They strongly believe that the woodshed, like the bedroom, is one place the government has no right to intrude. From long-standing tradition, Americans don't like to be told what they can or can't do behind the closed doors of our homes.

Countless times social workers hear of situations where well-intentioned persons wanted to do something to come to the aid of a child they believed to be suffering, but who hesitated because of the stronger fear of invading a family's privacy. To any thoughtful person, this need to act versus the need for family privacy can be a painful dilemma. Anyone who has been the subject of a child maltreatment investigation, whether substantiated or not, can speak of the fear, anger, anxiety and embarrassment that accompanies a police officer or social worker inquiring about what goes on in the "sanctity of the home."

Table 2: Assessment of the High-Risk Parent: Warning Signals*

I. *Historical Factors*

1. Missed or distorted attachment relationships in the parent's childhood.
2. Impaired intellectual or emotional functioning on the part of the parent.
3. Repeated exposure to parental rejection, hostility, and deprivation in parent's childhood.
4. Alternate exposure to deprivation and dependency during the parent's childhood.
5. Impaired ability to form relationships of any depth on the part of the parent (poor peer relationships and history of failed romantic relationships).
6. Historical pattern of self-imposed isolation and withdrawal from persons and events outside the nuclear family.
7. Demonstrated impairment in ability to trust; propensity to externalize blame *(distortion in trustability).*
8. Low self-esteem and self-confidence; pervasive anxiety and insecurity *(sense of personal inadequacy).*
9. Poor frustration tolerance, inability to delay gratification, poor impulse control *(weakened self-control).*
10. Absence of available social support and poor utilization of support when available *(inability to ask for help).*

II. *Environmental Factors*

1. Poverty or extreme financial insecurity. May be absence of financial resources or misuse of adequate resources.
2. Early marriage, marital distress, repetitive marital or marriage-like cohabitation during which the parent felt he was "taken advantage of" by his partner.
3. Early childbirth.
4. Frequent child birth; birth in rapid succession; presence of large number of children, which "overloads" physical and parenting environment.
5. Remarriage after childbirth with childbearing in new marriage. Places original child in jeopardy through Cinderella Effect.
6. Prematurely terminated education, sooner than desired.
7. Underemployment; participating in menial and frustrating job.
8. Ignorance of child development.
9. Ignorance of child-care necessities.
10. Adequate awareness of child development and parenting skills but refusal to employ this knowledge with the child.

---

*Frank G. Bolton, Jr., "From Theory to Practice," pp. 194–196, *When Bonding Fails: Clinical Assessment of High Risk Families*, Copyright © 1983 by Sage Publications. Reprinted with publisher's permission.

III. *Behavioral Factors*

1. Overt rejection of child at any stage.
2. Denial of pregnancy; failure to receive prenatal care, failure to prepare environment, failure to acquire necessary knowledge.
3. Distortions of pregnancy; absence of fantasy, rigid expectations of child in fantasy, seeking child to compensate for perceived emotional loss during childhood.
4. Negative reaction to childbirth; failure to respond to child, negative statements about child or father, absence of desire for contact, fear.
5. Postnatal disappointment or depression; ignoring child, child does not meet expectations, child is "taking advantage" of parent or fails to respond to parental needs and commands.
6. Rigid expectations of child that do not alter during first days of child care; inability to perceive child's helplessness.
7. Rejection of major child-care tasks; feeding, soothing, touching.
8. Perception of child as extension of the parent rather than as individual.
9. Inability to perceive child's behavior as rewarding.
10. Absence of reciprocal interaction between parent and child.
11. Inability to interpret child's cues and respond to the cues in a sensitive manner.
12. Perception of child as competitor for physical and emotional resources in the environment.
13. Requiring child to play parental (giving) roles.
14. Disallowing opportunity for relationships between the child and other persons.
15. Concentration on the external appearances of parenting: dressing the child, but not changing diapers, for example.
16. Absence of reaction to separation from the child; hands to strangers, does not keep child in sight, welcomes opportunity to focus attention on himself.

Table 3: Assessment of the High-Risk Child: Warning Signals

I. *Historical*

1. Product of difficult pregnancy.
2. Product of difficult delivery.
3. Infant with congenital anomalie, prematurity, or low birth weight.
4. Birth situation contributing to prolonged separation.
5. Factors contributing to difficulty in early care: prematurity neurological impairments, mismatching of parental and child stimulation levels.
6. Distortions in growth and development; failure to thrive.
7. Feeding difficulties.
8. Difficulty in soothability.
9. Perceived by parent as "difficult" child to care for or as "different" from siblings or other children.
10. Perceived by parent as having "something wrong" or not being "understandable" from the point of birth.

II. *Behavioral Factors*

1. Failure to reciprocate parental actions.
2. Failure to seek parental attention; withdrawn, lethargic.
3. Frightened, anxious, and insecure; over or under reactions to separation from parent.
4. Emotionally too "adult" for chronological age.
5. Distortions in affection; fear of love and affection despite obvious craving or indiscriminate affection.
6. Continuous seeking of parental approval.
7. Justification of parental actions; frequently accepting blame.
8. Lack of ability to trust.
9. Impaired self-esteem and self-confidence.
10. Waiting for his own parenthood to "make things all right."

When children are found dead, or run away, or kill their abusive parents because they know of no other way to end the abuse, the results of the community's failure to act become tragically evident. It is obvious that we must weigh the cost of absolute privacy of families against the right of children to safety and love. *Does the family's right to privacy outweigh the moral obligation to report risks to a child's life—not only physical, but emotional as well?*

To my mind, as soldiers on the front lines who see the casualties daily, the question is rhetorical. If we err, it should always be on the side of the child or anyone else who is helpless. Those who fear that violation of privacy and harassment by the social-legal system could result from such an interventionist view should realize that due process of law is designed to protect them from arbitrary and capricious action by service professionals. The rare individual or family unjustly charged for child neglect or abuse will survive and recover from the embarrassment. The child who is left to suffer because of reluctance to invade the family's privacy may not be so fortunate.

Can Abuse Be Predicted?

Unfortunately, no screening test has yet been developed that can predict child abuse. Countless theories have been developed to account for the outcomes; since the measure of a theory's value is its ability to predict better-than-chance estimates, these *post hoc* theories are not particularly helpful. As "resilient" children demonstrate, the incidence of maternal psychopathology, separation and loss, neglect, conflict and other negative factors does not necessarily mean pathology will develop in the child. Only overt rejection seems to hold the capacity for nearly universal disturbance in children.[9] The very same traumatic events or deficits that do produce maladaptation and illness in many people are also found among large numbers of normal individuals, who for reasons we have yet to learn, sustain these risks without significant impairment of personality development.

Nevertheless, the Tables 2 and 3 indicate widely accepted warning signals used to assess high-risk parents and children. Frank Bolton cautions that using these warning signals does not, per se, predict abuse,[10] but it helps identify the degree of risk. The parents at the highest risk may be beyond help, the ones at the lowest merely in need of prevention and educational services. Clinicians then can concentrate on the approximately eighty percent of families in the middle.

Since the progress with high-risk neglecting/absent parents is usually slow and effective only when preceeded by months of nurturance to the needy parents, efforts are best directed toward the children. As soon as children are identified as being at high risk, immediate intervention should begin, since the earlier in a child's life that intervention is begun, the greater is the likelihood of a normal life later.

Examining Our Own Behavior

A mother related the shock she felt at hearing herself on tape, screaming, threatening, and putting down her children. Her son had hidden a tape recorder where it picked up her reactions when she came home from work, after which he rather sheepishly played it for his mother. "I couldn't believe I really sounded like that. It made me think for awhile before I started yelling."

Experts suggest that parents periodically examine the behavior they exhibit to their children. If they identify unfair demands, frequent verbal putdowns, threatening, screaming and anger, perhaps family counseling or other help is warranted. If children's behaviors include lying, stealing, alcohol and drug usage, sneaking out, lack of impulse control, sudden and excessive mood swings, withdrawal and the like, parents might well question what role emotional maltreatment could be playing in the troublesome symptoms.

Hope exists for emotionally damaged children. Human beings are magnificently resilient. But nothing much will change until a concerted effort and willingness to spend dollars on research occurs. Prevention, not intervention, holds the key to breaking the circle.

Chapter Eleven

If I Were Starting My Family Again

High Self-Esteem for Children

Most of the anecdotes related to this point probably appear cruelly foreign to the type of relationships readers have experienced with children. The harsh rejection, spirit-crushing ridicule and other types of punishing behaviors detailed may seem so remote that they have little bearing on the lives of parents and others who truly love children. Yet for most people reading this book, the absence of a maltreatment pattern is not enough for them. We wish for children *optimal* treatment, the best we can give them.

As a family social worker, I have a tendency to constantly check out the emotional health of my children and our parental relationship to them. Like the legendary shoemaker's children who go barefoot, I occasionally fear my own children will not be perfectly adjusted (whatever that means); that I'm too strict or too lenient; that I expect too much or not enough, and so on.

I expect far more of myself as a parent than merely not maltreating my children. I challenge myself to raise children who are caring, responsible, contributing individuals, ones who feel good about themselves. As I've searched for ways to encourage children's well-being, one quality has consistently emerged as being the foundation of those other desirable qualities. That quality is self-esteem.

In a very real way, like emotional maltreatment, an individual's worth is of concern to the whole society. The health of an entire society depends on the personal worth of every member. Whenever society denies worth to large numbers of people, that society suffers. In late twentieth-century America, people who are not young, beautiful, rich, successful and thin are not valued much. Advertising and the media promulgate the notion that self-esteem is contingent on such externals, and society today pays the price in countless ways.

The insecurity that appears in such diverse disorders as neo-Nazism, alcohol and drug abuse, neuroticism, family violence and social unrest attest to the pain of people feeling unloved and unimportant. While no individual can rebuild the world, we can help our children to have the inner strength to cope with it more successfully. I suggest several ways of helping children to gain that inner strength, to encourage their high self-esteem.

In the course of reading countless books on self-esteem and parenting, one gets the distinct impression that a child's self-esteem, or lack of it, lies entirely with her parents. One misstep, one cross word, one incident of ignoring the child, and self-esteem goes down the tubes forever. What guilt this approach exacts from people who, because they are human, sometimes fail to show the love they feel!

I've been fortunate to get to know hundreds of children fairly well during the last twenty years. Being mother to three of my own children, I can see firsthand how different congenital temperaments affect children's self-esteem. Factors totally outside of parental control, such as peer acceptance or rejection, handicapping conditions and so on, can have a powerful effect on how children feel about themselves.

My experiences lead me to believe that the unrelieved picture of model parental behavior held up to parents as an ideal for which they should strive is discouraging and unrealistic. It is a contrived picture, the picture of a parent who never ever says or does anything regrettable. And it is false. The suggestion that a carelessly spoken word or an angry, resentful glance will forever damage the child must be laid to rest.

All the same, few experts deny that parents' actions and attitudes as expressed in daily living, not isolated instances, are the largest single factor in determining the child's self-esteem. That self-esteem has to do, not only with how children feel about themselves, but how they face the world. People who have high self-esteem develop skills and attitudes that help them to accomplish their goals and deal with frustrations. How to help children gain high levels of esteem is a challenge every loving parent tries to meet; some do a more effective job than others.

In writing this chapter, I decided to go straight to the experts. I asked my own children, as well as those of friends, to name one thing parents can do to make their children feel good about themselves. ("You mean develop self-esteem?" asked Erik, my fifteen-year-old son, wise in the vocabulary of social workers.) The following strategies for parents were specified by these young experts. They are attitudes I would strive to achieve if I were starting my family again.

1. Praise when appropriate; don't ridicule when offering criticism.

Praise is probably one of those techniques that most people think of as a way to show support. That does not mean we put that knowledge into practice. Most of us fall into the pattern of taking our good feelings about children for granted, not verbalizing or acting on them through smiles, touches and other nonverbal ways. At the same time, we seldom forget to express our negative feelings in explicit detail. Rather than making a point of mentioning every way we're disappointed in the shortcomings of our children, we can try to emphasize the positive. "In praising and loving a child," said Goethe, "we love and praise not that which is, but that which we hope for."

Children do not take positive feelings from parents for granted, especially when most of what they hear from them are either commands to do something or scoldings for something they should not have done. Kids need to hear and see from our smiles and body language that we think they are good, special, fantastic. And they need to hear it often!

While the emphasis on communicating positive feelings toward children can hardly be overstated, this does not mean that verbal praise should be laid on with a trowel. Praise should be specific and used judiciously. When it's specific, it's more believable and can be used as a self-esteem raising technique. Even small children can tell if they are being flattered or manipulated by false praise.

Real praise by comparison, reflects what we feel about the child, as well as about her actions. The experts who suggest never, ever praising children for their performance lest they decide we love them only when they do well, do not seem to live in a real world. The real world *does* value performance, and to suggest to a child that nothing much is expected does not produce self-esteem.

When the need to criticize behavior arises, do it in a way that concentrates on that behavior, not the person. Correct in a way that does not ridicule or humiliate the child. Even "praise" can be used in a sarcastic way that suggests past failures. Comments such as, "For a girl you're good at math," or "For a fat person you don't sweat much" are not praise.

A good rule of thumb in using praise to boost self-esteem is to describe instead of evaluate. Describing what you see or feel, rather than judging it, is a technique Dr. Thomas Gordon advocates in his book *Parent Effectiveness Training.*

There are many other ways to minimize the likelihood that necessary punishment will lead to lowered self-esteem in children. Statements that correct behavior should be done privately, away from other children, and they should offer suggestions as to how, specifically, the behavior should be changed. Especially with very young kids, it's easy to assume they automatically know what should be done differently.

While everyone has inherent dignity, if it isn't honored by others, it can become lost. If we remember that children are *persons* with feelings and needs, we'll be more likely to treat them with a dignity that builds self-respect and a willingness to respond to others in a positive way.

The second expert I interviewed, was my teenage daughter Katie.

2. Help your child deal with adversity.

"Help kids who get teased about their appearance to cope." That was how she put it.

Some charmed children may go blissfully through life, serenely unaffected by characteristics of ridicule, such as protruding teeth or obesity, but few will escape an unsympathetic world at one point or another in their lives. In a society that increasingly seems to judge people by how they look and perform, parents would be naive to underestimate the effect a child's peers have on his self-esteem. Although the parents may like to believe that they alone lay the foundations for their children's self-esteem, by the time children enter school, the peer group exerts a powerful influence. Many times these other children will not be as kind in their words and actions as parents. We cannot possibly prevent the kinds of social problems that our children may have to face, and, in fact, it probably wouldn't be advisable. If the child's adversity is not so great that it is crushing, in later years it can make a secure and confident adult, one who is comfortable in dealing with other problems that inevitably come to us all.

What makes the difference in the life of a child who is overwhelmed by a sense of inferiority and self-hatred, and the child who learns to overcome? If we look again at studies of resilient children we see that despite many obstacles, these children learned to *compensate.*

Unfortunately, heroes and heroines are somewhat out of fashion today. The idols of most children are packaged by imagemakers, and few have anything to tell our youngsters about overcoming any adversity other than low ratings on the top forty or a batting slump. In the past, children who were forced to cope with adversity maintained as heroes people who had learned to compensate for their adversity. Eleanor Roosevelt, Thomas Edison, Abraham Lincoln, Helen Keller, Jim Thorpe, to name only a few, compensated for handicaps and physical unattractiveness, rising over their failings like the legendary phoenix.

As adults who care, we can help children to develop strengths and talents that counterbalance those weaknesses which might otherwise crush self-esteem. The child who has a learning disability, who is too tall, who has a birthmark, who feels "average"; all of them need to find an area in which they can feel adequate and self-confident. Music, art, cooking, sports, storytelling—the possibilities are endless.

One tactic often used in coping with adversity or stress of any kind is the use of humor. Norman Cousins in his widely read *Anatomy of an Illness,* describes how he learned that laughter really is the best medicine. A family that helps its members laugh with each other and shares humor at their own expense will be giving children a good weapon to use against feelings of inferiority imposed by others.

3. Treat children with respect and insist they do the same for others.

Families that produce children with high self-esteem don't allow members to "put down" others or treat each other disrespectfully. If kids are to respect others, they need to have known respect from parents. They need the safety of knowing that they are accepted for what they are.

Although as parents we may love our children dearly, it is sometimes easy to forget to treat them like persons, and we often say things in their presence we wouldn't dream of uttering if that child were a grown friend.

"Janelle looks just like her father," a woman told me a short time ago. Janelle, humiliated and wishing she were somewhere else, hung her head. "I just hope she doesn't end up like him. He's a good-for-nothing; I haven't heard from him in years." That kind of insensitivity to children's feelings shows disrespect that does not build self-esteem.

Treating children respectfully means being fair with them. It means we will have realistic ideas about what they're capable of doing. It means we will show interest in opinions and decision-making, even if we don't agree. It means speaking as politely to children as we expect them to speak to us. We won't permit belittling or abusive language or ordering others about. We won't bring up children's mistakes and faults as topics of conversations with others, or use them as the butt of our jokes. All these disrespectful actions erode a child's self-esteem and will probably help produce a disrespectful child.

Merely because parents model respect for each other and their children does not ensure that children will return that respect. Turn on almost any current television family situation comedy and you will see a smart-mouthed kid or two and rather befuddled parents who make no motions to gain the respect due them. I have dealt with real-life families similar to this where one parent, generally the mother, tolerates unbelievable language and derogatory actions from children. These mothers weakly roll their eyes as if to say, "Look what I have to put up with."

Parents and other adults should never let children get away with disrespectful talk. We must insist on courtesy and consideration not only for our own sake, but for the children's. Once a pattern of insolence is established, breaking it can be hard.

To really get across to a child that you will not put up with disrespect, you may need to take drastic action, such as refusing to perform services taken for granted (laundry, transportation or even cooking.) If parents don't insist on being treated kindly by their children, other authorities, such as teachers and police, are not likely to get their respect either.

Teach your children that "putting down" their brothers, sisters and friends is likewise unacceptable. Parents should make clear their disapproval of any form of disrespect, regardless of to whom it is directed. Working with teenagers, I see the destructive and pervasive effects of kids cruelly cutting each other down—even their friends. At the time when, as teenagers, they are most vulnerable and most need to hear good things about themselves, they systematically destroy each others' self-esteem. While adults cannot prevent this from happening altogether, they can help kids understand how damaging this disrespect can be.

4. Help children to develop a sense of competence.

Think back if you can to a time you watched the first triumphant steps of a baby walking alone. Think of the tremendous exultation and joy reflected in the child. That sense of "What a wonderful feeling; I can do it!" can be fostered in children of all ages by adults.

Children who are encouraged to feel competent learn very early that they can influence what happens in their lives. They know that their skills will be sufficient for the tasks life presents them, or at least know how to get the resources that they need. They know that they have something to offer others.

Parents and others can use several approaches to help children feel competent. We can set up situations that help the child to succeed. When still very young, the environment can be adapted so that most frustrations are minimized. As the child attempts imperfectly to try different activities, parents and others can offer praise for what has been accomplished, rather than scold for what did not get done.

When children do fail, parents can help them cope. Far worse than failing at something is the fear of trying again lest failure result. Children who learn to take reasonable risks and to handle failure when it occurs grow in self-esteem. Adults can help kids to deal positively with failure in several ways: by analyzing the experience with older children so that it need not be repeated; by helping them set reasonable, as opposed to impossible, standards; and, above all, by treating failure as something that happened rather than as a personal characteristic.

Another method for developing children's sense of competence is to provide reasonable rules. When children know the limits, they feel more secure. As children learn to follow these guidelines, they learn to develop responsibility and make good decisions. Children given the chance to make decisions about noncritical areas which affect them gain a sense of competence and self-esteem.

This type of decisionmaking, it is emphasized, should not be the inappropriate role-reversed decision-making thrust upon children by parents who depend on their children. Rather, it should be the kind that gives them an opportunity to be involved in matters affecting them. Choosing among options for a family outing, or picking out colors for the bedroom, for example, are decisions suitable for young children's influence.

Allowing children to make some decisions doesn't mean that every issue need come to a vote. It does mean that even though parents are in charge, children's opinions count.

Remember, too, that when children are involved in competitive activities, personal worth doesn't hinge on how well one person does at another's expense. Emphasize the effort, not the winning or losing.

Try not to impose your own desire to be a winner on your child. Your own unfulfilled dreams of being a prima ballerina or home run king shouldn't diminish your youngsters' pleasure in participation. Competition should boost self-esteem, not reduce it.

5. Don't compare children to others.

A woman once told me bitterly that she had always lived in the shadow of her older sister who, in the eyes of her parents, was beautiful, smart and sociable: everything the parents constantly reminded the younger sister she was not. Most adults are probably more subtle than that, but still they can make implied or explicit comparisons between children. If they are made to children outside the family, they can be irritating. If the comparisons are made to siblings by parents, they can be devastating and lead to intense resentment or jealousy of the praised brother or sister.

In homes where, because of divorce, children do not live with both parents, the custodial parent may harp on a child's undesirable traits "inherited" from the absent parent. The message comes to the child: "You're just as irresponsible (or dishonest, or lazy) as your father. You'll turn out to be just like him. A failure." If comparisons are made at all, make them positive ones.

Related to the idea of not comparing children with each other is the importance of treating sons and daughters equally. A while ago I remember reading an article entitled "Son Worship" in which the author commented on the way some mothers make martyrs of themselves, waiting on every whim of their sons, while daughters are expected to pull more than their fair share. She observed that a man brought up by a mother who never expected him to pick up his dirty socks or wash out the bathtub after himself will not be easy to change after marriage.[2]

This discrimination leads boys to grow up thinking that they have the right to expect women to pick up after them, and it teaches girls that they are meant to go through life doing what men needn't do. It strips both sexes of real self-esteem.

The other side of the coin is that we may shower little girls with far more touching and cuddling, and from an early age, make little boys into "little men" who should show little emotion.

6. Cherish your children.

One of the most moving experiences of my life was the week I spent with a foster child who was being evaluated at Children's Hospital in Denver. Babies and small children, most of them desperately sick, filled the ward. Laurie, one such three year old, lay weakly in a crib close to where Elizabeth, my foster baby, stayed when not being tested elsewhere. Her mother kept a constant vigil, stroking her daughter's skin, gazing lovingly into her eyes, humming softly and endlessly whispering endearments to her. The mother, who had dark circles under her eyes and moved as though she carried the weight of the world, left each day only long enough to shower and change her clothes.

For five days I watched her hover over her child, realizing from the nurses' averted eyes and meaningful looks at each other that the end was near for Laurie. The fifth day, Laurie's mother pulled her chair over to mine. Tears streaming down her cheeks, she took my hand and squeezed it. She spoke with urgency. "I hope your baby knows you love her. Laurie really never knew I loved her till it was too late."

Early the next morning when I arrived from the motel, Laurie was gone, her crib stripped and scrubbed. The chair where her mother had sat was pushed against the wall. No vestige of either remained. Yet that grieving woman's words have stayed with me.

When I see people belittling and humiliating their children, ignoring them, jerking them roughly about or treating them with contempt, I think of her words. Why does it so often take a crisis in the lives of our children for us to cherish them in the way they deserve?

Cherish is one of those words like "duty" and "honor" that has an old-fashioned sound to it. I can think of no better word to convey the sense of delight and wonder that *those* children are *our* children. Parents who cherish their children, while occasionally losing their tempers at them, let the children know they consider them marvels. While becoming irritated at them, the parents still let the children know how wonderful they are. These parents are continuously refreshed by the wonder of what their kids think and feel and say and do. The children who have cherishing parents know that they are the best things that ever happened to their parents!

Dorothy Corkille Briggs, author of *Your Child's Self-Esteem,* writes, "If I were to treat my friends as I treat my children, how many friends would I have left? Few of us would think of shaming or analyzing friends in front of others, jerking them up short with sarcasm, humiliating, embarrassing, hitting or ordering them about like soldiers under our command. Of course not . . . Repeatedly, we treat children like second-class creatures devoid of feelings and yet, we prize them!"[3]

One of the best ways to show how much we care about children is to take them seriously and accept their feelings. Most people don't practice that, but instead deny kids' feelings or "talk down" to them. How often do you catch yourself saying things like "That's no reason to get upset," or "You can't possibly be too warm. Put your sweater back on."

Steady denial of feelings can confuse and anger anyone, especially children who may learn to distrust their feelings. When we deny children's feelings, we teach them to rely on someone else's judgment; it's certainly not a way to make them feel special.

It may be easy to learn how to say, "You're upset about losing the game" or "I'm feeling cold, but you must be feeling warmer." It's harder to react positively to statements like these: "I hate the baby. I wish he'd die," or "I'm really mad. The teacher gave me a failing grade just because I didn't get the stupid paper in on time."

The first type of response that usually comes to us is, "How awful. Of course you love that baby," or "You have no right to get angry if you got your paper in late." It's much easier to be accepting of feelings when they don't touch areas of our lives that make us angry or defensive. Then it's hard not to revert to denial of those feelings.

(Note: While all feelings can be accepted and acknowledged, certain actions must be limited. You can teach the child that while anger is legitimate, poking someone in the nose is not.)

Think about your own reaction if a well-intentioned friend told you that you shouldn't feel worried or angry or blue. The last thing I want to hear when I'm in any of these moods is amateur psychology, advice, or denial of my feelings. Since most of us grew up having feelings denied, effort is required to help children recognize and deal with their feelings.

Instead of interrupting with analysis or denial, listen with full attention, acknowledging feelings when children are through talking. Try to tune into the feelings and use words such as "Oh" and "I see." These words, coupled with attention and a caring attitude give children strength and a sense of how they are cherished. When we acknowledge their feelings without moralizing or denying, we give them confidence in an inner reality, one of the roots of self-esteem.

There is probably not a parent who doesn't occasionally get preachy and judgmental. While this needn't make us feel guilty, we can resolve to be more open in our communication with children. One good way to do this is to send "I-messages" instead of "you-messages." "You-messages" evaluate, criticize and point out failings. "I-messages" emphasize feelings and reactions.

Imagine your children acting boisterously and shouting at each other as you try to read in the same room. Your first reaction may be to shout too. "You kids are really wild. Settle down right now."

If instead you send an "I-message," their interpretation will be closer to what you probably really feel about them, and their self-esteem will not be damaged. "I'm trying to read this article, but it's too noisy for me to concentrate" doesn't suggest, as the "you-message" can, that there's something basically wrong with the kids. The difference between "I-" and "you-messages", in capsule form, is that the former describes feelings while the latter lays blame, and blame-laying is not a good way to build self-esteem.

7. Be consistent in rules and attitudes.

Last Saturday, Katie, who was in a hurry to get to her friend's house and who didn't finish one of her chores, left a bathroom floor unswept and unscrubbed. I didn't say anything to her, because I was busy with my own activities and in an upbeat frame of mind.

This Saturday, however, things had not gone so well for me. I was short-tempered and when, once again, she didn't do her chores to my expectations, I got angry. "What's the matter with you? I've taught you to do better work than that," I shouted at her.

Since I'd ignored the problem the week before, Katie's failure to finish the job was partly my fault. My lack of consistency did not let her know exactly what I expected of her.

It is extreme inconsistency, however, that is truly damaging. Although children can learn to adapt to, and even thrive under, incredibly varied conditions, they are basically conservative and need a consistent presentation of reality. Extreme inconsistency gives little definition of what is right and wrong, what standards are, what is expected or how social relationships develop.

Consistency gives children welcome boundaries. When they are older, they can choose different standards or types of relationships, but in the beginning they need consistency if they are to develop normally. In today's rapidly changing society with its uncertainty about values, consistency in standards and behavior is needed more than ever before in the lives of children.

8. Make time for children.

Making time for children every day tells them in a special way how precious they are to you. If we wait to "find" time those special moments will seldom or never occur. Time with children needs to be planned. One woman saves her dusting for a time when her daughter comes home from school. She knows she can do that while paying attention to her child and sharing the day's activities with her.

While planned times with children are important, we should be careful not to choose times that neither parent or child will enjoy. No matter how much I might want to talk to my son Erik early in the morning, it is not a "good time" for me because I am a slow-waker. It would not be a good experience for either of us if I tried to force my attention on him before eight a.m.

If certain shared activities leave parent or child feeling martyred, look for others. Children can pick up on parental enthusiasm or faking. Find things to do that everyone can enjoy, even if it's as simple as walking together or sharing work. One evening we all peeled and sliced apples, then made pies for the freezer, an activity that made me wonder why we don't try to do more of our work together.

Develop traditions for spending time both at holidays and ordinary times. Rituals as simple as always making homemade valentines for family members, putting up the tree the Sunday before Christmas, spending Labor Day washing and putting up storm windows, tie the family together. The great value of rituals such as these is that they give the child a sense of identity and belonging. As with consistency, in a society that works against stability, rituals strengthen both the family and individual's self-esteem.

Another time that it's important to be with children is when they're sick. If both parents are employed, whenever possible, they should take time off to be with ill children. They are particularly vulnerable then, and time willingly spent with them suggests, like no other way, how special they are.

Countless means exist to help children develop high self-esteem. Above all, enjoying children and letting them know how much we enjoy them will strengthen them to deal with whatever lies ahead.

Chapter Twelve

Changing Pictures

Nurturing Personal Self-Esteem

"I've never felt good about myself. I don't believe I'm loveable and I mistrust anyone who seems to like me. All through my years growing up I learned from my parents and teachers that I had a lot of things wrong with me. "You're not good at anything" was mostly what I heard.

"When I became a teenager, my worst fear was that no one would marry me. I guess I grabbed onto the first offer I got, getting married for all the wrong reasons. I'm still in a loveless marriage, but feel rotten about myself, and it's rubbing off on my children. I find myself shaming and critizing them constantly. I worry about how what I'm doing to them will affect their lives. Is their anything I can do to change?"

These were the words of a well-dressed, well-off homemaker. Her swollen, tear-stained face presented a jarring contrast to her immaculate grooming and the image of a happy wife and mother seen by most people. Underneath her expensive clothing and artfully-applied makeup was a scared little girl desperately trying to be good enough, neat enough and smart enough to gain her parents' love. The withheld affection never came though, and Suzanne is still vainly trying to measure up, to feel good about herself.

As pointed out, parents' own sense of inferiority makes it difficult for them to accept imperfection in their children. They don't intend to reject

155

their children, and like Suzanne, work hard at concealing these feelings even from themselves. When imperfect children (is there any other kind?) inadvertently remind parents of their personal fears and inadequacies, those bad feelings get transferred to the children or to the child that most reminds the parent of his own hated personal qualities. As part of the strategy for breaking the circle of child abuse, it is crucial to raise individual parents' own self-esteem.

Study after study shows that parents who mistreat their children have low self-esteem, so low that they use their children in an attempt to feel better about themselves. That doesn't work, and after mistreating them, the parents' self-esteem sinks lower still. The stage is set for more abuse or neglect.

We realize this connection between how we feel ourselves and how we act to others. If we feel unimportant, incompetent or unloved, we are likely to want to kick the dog or yell at the kids. By taking responsibility for our own self-esteem, we not only feel better ourselves, but we will raise our children with higher self-esteem.

But taking this responsibility is not easy. It's scary to take charge. It's easier to keep hoping that someone—or something else—will somehow magically convey a sense of personal worth to us. For many women, especially women who endure abuse at the hands of their husbands, self-esteem is tied to the requirement that men must find them desirable. For those men, it is tied to a sense of control over people who are weaker than themselves. These are unsatisfactory bases for self-esteem, since the real thing comes from within, from knowing our own loveability and capability. Fortunate children grow up knowing self-esteem from their parents. What about those parents who may have a sense of personal inadequacy, who grew up with disgrace and ridicule shaping the picture of themselves they carry around in their heads?

Changing the Picture You Carry

Like most parents, I carry in my wallet pictures of my children. Sometimes a year or more goes by without my having really looked at those pictures. Then, perhaps while visiting with a new acquaintance, talking about my family, I pull out their school photos and invariably say something to the effect that "These are old pictures. The children have changed a lot since they were taken." When I get back home, if I remember, I replace the old photos with new ones.

Our internal pictures of ourselves also need to be periodically taken out and examined, and replaced, if necessary. If you grew up exposed to put-downs and derision, you have an internal picture of yourself as a child that reflects those attitudes. If you grew up hearing and believing you were a nifty kid, one who was loveable and made a difference in people's lives, you have a much more favorable picture of yourself in your head. Whatever opinions or attitudes you developed because of how you were treated early in life gelled into conclusions that are seen as being accurate, regardless of the facts. Any qualities not fitting with that picture are filtered out and rejected.

Within his first five or six years of life, Jamie, the victim of PSD described in Chapter Seven, formed a picture of himself as being "the baddest kid." This picture was based on the messages he received from parents, neighbors and, perhaps, even the school. Much later, praise and the other positive messages we tried using to change his self-image were rejected in no uncertain terms. His picture was created in such a way that qualities, such as obedience and kindness, had no place. Jamie's behavior as an out-of-control ten year old matched the picture he'd put together in his head years earlier.

Jamie's picture, though well-defined, was a recent one. For a person who has lived enough years to have that internal picture yellowed and frayed around the edges, changing the self-image can be difficult. Some people don't even know that it's possible to change their pictures. Others may know it can be done, but don't want to change enough to go through the effort involved.

What are some of the common self pictures people carry around that profoundly affect the way children are treated?

Picture of a Lonely Child

If you feel you don't really belong, or are only loosely attached to people you care about, you may be overly concerned about getting the love you "deserve" from your child. Statements the child might make in anger such as "I hate you, Mom," can be totally devastating. Parents who carry around a picture of themselves as not belonging can be excessively worried about their children's relationship to themselves and others, getting into the right social groups, a prestige school or occupation, and so on. A parent who carries an old internal picture that shows a child standing apart from everyone else often tries too hard to push her own children into belonging.

Some parents I work with, who see themselves as isolated and nonattached, show the opposite behavior. They are the parents who neglect their children, avoiding involvement. They seem to care little how the children feel or what they are doing. These are parents that teachers cannot get to school for conferences, and that doctors find do not carry through on medical treatment. Involvement is as short or infrequent as the parent can manage to make it. Parents such as these may have learned very early in life not to bother trying to get close to people. They may have never learned to trust others and withdraw emotionally from anyone who can hurt them.

Picture of a Dull Child

A second picture of themselves that many people carry is that of a child who is boring, dumb or dull. These people don't see their own uniqueness or special qualities, and often try desperately to blend in with the crowd. "Keeping up with the Joneses" can become an obsession.

If you carry the picture of a child who is dumb or boring, you may avoid doing anything to draw attention to yourself, and suffer from embarrassment and confusion if attention becomes focused on you in public. Instead of developing qualities that make you special, you probably seldom take pride or delight in what you have produced. "What? This dress? Anyone could make it," is the type of disparaging comment frequently made by people who have problems seeing how unique they really are.

Parents who carry this old picture of themselves may have problems with children who are imaginative or "different" because of appearance, disabling conditions and other behavior. This may show up in relationships with children in a variety of ways, but most often it results in attempts to suppress a youngster's uniqueness. Statements such as "You don't see anyone else doing that (wearing that, etc.)" are common. Conformity, at all costs, is frequent in parents who grew up lacking a sense of being special or unique.

Picture of a Helpless Child

A third, and probably the most common, internal picture adults carry is one of a helpless, powerless child who has no control over events or circumstances. They see life as "just happening" to them, and they don't take responsibility for their actions. Adults who see themselves in this manner blame others for things that are clearly their own fault; see themselves as being incompetent in areas in which they clearly should be competent; do not finish jobs; and often are emotionally unstable, easily crying, getting angry and hysterical.

In attempts to achieve some degree of control in their lives, such people often act inappropriately. They may be bossy and aggressive, insist on doing things beyond their capabilities, then fail, while simultaneously avoiding doing things at which they could be competent. They often are unpleasant to be around because of loud voices and threatening body language that intimidates others. People who try to use these methods are often considered bullies as children, and, as parents, they continue to bully their own children by dominating them through verbal and physical attacks.

Parents who feel "not in charge" may find it difficult to set consistent limits for children. Depending on the intensity of helpless feelings, they may be extremely demanding and controlling or very permissive.

When people feel helpless, they look to others, including their children, not only for power, but for happiness. Jokes about "Jewish mothers" are really comments on all parents who feel powerless and attempt to use guilt or verbal manipulation to obtain personal satisfaction. Children who buy into this scheme are made to feel responsible for keeping parents happy, well, sane, or whatever other condition is imposed upon them.

If you happen to have one of these internal pictures that chips away at your self-esteem, you may unconsciously act today in ways that reinforce that picture. If you carry the picture of yourself as a child who just didn't belong or fit in, you may allow job, social or other pressures to keep you from making adequate time for your spouse and children.

Your marriage may not be as good as you'd like it to be; conversations may focus almost entirely on the mechanisms of running a home: what to buy, what needs fixing, what to do about children's behavior. Little intimacy exists when one or both partners lack a sense of belonging.

Members of families in which parents lack a sense of belonging all tend to go their own way, finding little time to share feelings or activities with each other or the entire group.

Change is threatening and people who think themselves dull will endure considerable pain rather than risk new ways of thinking or doing. Within the family, little emotion is expressed. Seldom is spontaneous joy, excitement or elation verbalized. Life seems to always go along on the same humdrum level. Instead of identifying feelings, family members may daydream and fantasize like Thurber's Walter Mitty.

If you carry around the picture of a helpless child, you may have problems controlling your feelings and get into trouble for outbursts with family and coworkers. Once begun, you may have problems finishing projects, or feel as though you are always getting blamed for other people's actions. A good deal of the time you may feel taken advantage of and avoid making decisions. Procrastination and always being a little late are your trademarks.

Changing Pictures

What can be done if you recognize yourself as at least occasionally carrying any of these pictures, and want to put it away for one that's newer and more like you'd prefer seeing yourself?

I wish I could explain *one, two, three,* how a person could quickly and easily dispose of a poor self-image and achieve a shiny new one. Unfortunately, like "get rich"- or "get thin quick" books, any such formula is pretty much worthless. The truth is that, for most people, personal change comes hard and rather slowly. If you are sufficiently motivated to go about changing your self-image, you can do so. In some cases, you may need professional help. But fortunately, for most people, psychoanalysis is unnecessary. *Self-examination is not.*

One of the areas we need to examine is how we meet our psychological needs. Many of us believe that satisfaction of these needs depends on outside persons or events: friends, success in school or at work, one's husband or wife, children, and so on. As long as we do not take responsibility for getting our own psychological needs met, we may wait for that magical someone or something to comfort and nurture us. When this person or event doesn't materialize, or doesn't do the job adequately, resentment and further deterioration of self-esteem occurs. Instead of vainly hoping, we can take charge of our lives. Waiting for someone to do something for us that we should be doing for ourselves contributes to the lessening of our self-esteem.

Knowing that we alone are responsible for our emotional well-being and *doing something about it* are two very different things. People who discover I did graduate work in psychology are quick to tell me of psychologists or psychiatrists they have known who are crazy, maladjusted, suicidal, and so on. Clearly, intellectual knowledge does not of itself make a difference in people's attitudes and behaviors.

Part of self-examination includes accepting yourself as you are, including the parts you'd rather no one knew about, even yourself. We who are civilized, respectable people like to believe that we have no dark sides, that all primitive savagery long ago disappeared. In fact, all those qualities and feelings are repressed in our unconscious minds where they reside just as vitally as ever.

Dr. William Miller observes, "Throughout much of the modern church, such stress has been placed on the development of goodness and righteousness *per se* that even the mere mention among Christian people of that which is dark and shadowy often seems out of place . . . it is my observation that substantially more harm is done by denying and repressing the shadow (the negative tendencies within us) than by coming to grips with it. Those who deny their shadows only project their evil onto others and see it there. Those who repress their shadows to maintain their purity and innocence are sometimes overcome by them and swept away in their very own evil." [1]

By acknowledging all of ourselves, even those parts we'd rather not admit, we are better able to start taking care of ourselves. Once we have come to know ourselves and have taken on the responsibility for meeting personal emotional needs, we can begin nurturing ourselves. This does not mean that we become self-centered hedonists who give into every whim and impulse. Instead, a person who truly nurtures herself, like a good and loving parent, realizes that setting limits and using self-discipline are frequently the caring and responsible actions to take. Saying "no" to destructive patterns, such as chronic belittling of one's self, drug and alcohol abuse and promiscuity, produces growth. Self-nurturing can mean saying "yes" to others' needs, forgiving yourself after you've taken responsibility for your mistakes, taking good care of yourself and the like.

Learning to nurture yourself and take responsibility for meeting your own emotional needs takes retraining. If you have fallen into harsh, critical ways of looking at yourself because of the early picture you were given by your parents, teachers or others, you'll probably need to learn new skills.

One of these skills is to converse with the inner critic that seeks to command or instill guilt. If you hear yourself saying, "I'm no good," "I'm inferior to other people," "No one loves me," and the like, you can learn to respond to those old voices that destroy self-esteem. By trying to recognize the truth, you can answer your negative voices and put them in perspective.

As an example, in reaction to a voice telling you that you are a rotten mother, you can write out the event you believe caused that perception. ("I lost my temper with Travis, I ignored Lucy and felt like punching Tom.") Then respond with a list of positive qualities, one you believe are truthful. ("I'm a good mother most of the time. I read to Travis today. I apologized to Lucy and told her I love her; Tom and I had fun tonight when I was bathing him.")

This exercise may seem foolish, but probably needs to be repeated dozens of times before you begin to change your thinking and locate the source of the unrealistic messages that repress your self-esteem.

Another type of language to watch out for are *shoulds*. For people who have no conscience or morality, people we call sociopaths, *shoulds* mean nothing. For most people, *shoulds* are basic rules that exist to protect the rights of all people. You *should* stop at red lights. You *should* pay taxes. You *should* treat your children with love and protection.

People with high self-esteem do not operate primarily by *shoulds*, but rather by a religious faith or code of ethics. Their lives are not controlled by *shoulds:* "I *should* lose weight." "I *should* read the classics." "I *should* save some money." "I *should* floss my teeth." This sort of barrage goes on for many of us all day and increases our feelings of inadequacy.

Since many of these *shoulds* are of themselves good, you can retrain yourself to send the messages without reducing your self-worth. Use words like prefer, wish, or choose instead. This may seem like a hairsplitting approach, but to a person whose self-esteem is low because of feelings of powerless, it can make a difference. *Should* and its relatives, *ought, must and have to,* are self-critical words. Prefer, wish and choose, on the other hand, imply self-control. These words do not mean that you sit back and do nothing. Instead, they imply being in charge and taking personal responsibility for actions.

Another way to take charge of meeting your own emotional needs as a way of raising self-esteem is to find possible role models. Dozens of good books are written every year that suggest ways of dealing with the specific issues that may contribute to your self-esteem being lower than you'd like it to be. Watch people who seem to carry positive internal pictures, and ask them how they have come to feel good about themselves.

One of the points of my personal philosophy about high self-esteem is that, to a point, it comes from reaching out to others. This reaching out, if genuinely motivated, does not leave you feeling burdened, unappreciated or resentful. The psychological truth of Jesus' words, "Whoever tries to save his own life will lose it; whoever loses his life will save it" (Luke 17:33) has been demonstrated through the years. The people who most frantically pursue happiness and self-esteem find that it eludes them; those who concentrate on reaching out to others achieve it unself-consciously.

For starters in reaching out, try some of the following:

1. an appreciative letter to someone you remember from your youth;
2. an invitation to lunch for someone having a bad day;
3. a gentle touch on someone's shoulder or elbow;
4. an unexpected gift for your husband or wife;
5. passing along a compliment to the person it concerned;
6. a leisurely walk with someone needing to get out;
7. a visit to a sick or elderly person who is confined to bed;
8. a soft word to someone who is angry;
9. a note of appreciation to your pastor or rabbi, doctor or dentist, children's principal or teacher;
10. genuine, focused concentration when someone talks to you;
11. sharing someone's pain or fear *without* embarrassment or judgment and maybe *with* tears.

You may feel you have lived too many years with a sad, torn picture of yourself to change it. Please reconsider that position. The human spirit is virtually indestructible and for your sake and that of your children, the possibility of health and vitality remains as long as the body draws breath.

The Last Word

This summer I saw my children go off in different directions for several weeks. "Write soon," "Remember I love you," "Call collect if you miss your connecting flight," and other words of love and admonition kept coming from me until at last only waves and kisses through a window were possible.

It's hard for me to say goodbye at the end of a book, too. I would like to go on, relating more true stories of children whose maimed spirits have touched my life, pleading for recognition of the extent of the problem, and for action and research to break the circle. I would like, too, to encourage parents, teachers, and anyone else who comes in contact with children to try to bring out their best.

We do want the best for them: enjoyment and effectiveness in their work, play, and love; an attitude that looks ahead with hope and self-confidence; self-esteem and a sense of being able to control events rather than being victims of them; self-discipline, honesty and faithfulness; adaptability and creativity; a sense of peace with themselves and others.

Books such as this one would have been unnecessary in the past. Learning how to live a useful and satisfying life, and developing the qualities to do so, came from family or perhaps the church. Most often the teaching was unspoken. There was no need for words. The teachings were commonly accepted and modeled by the vast majority of the society. There was no need for schools to teach how to cope or delay gratification; they could concentrate on academic knowledge. After all, the most important knowledge—that of knowing how to live happily and at peace with oneself and the world—is best taught, not in school, but in the family.

In today's tumultuous society, many families simply do not have the stability and warmth to teach those most important of skills, and a vicious circle is created. As I have tried to point out, parents have a difficult time teaching their children what they have themselves never learned. Until we know more about how parent-child relationships work, and how we can strengthen them, we will stumble along as a society, often misusing or abusing our most precious resource, our children.

Every adult reading this has the ability to help break the circle of abuse. Every one of us can help make a happier, healthier world for children and adults. By offering a helping hand, an empathetic word, a kind deed, such as babysitting for overtired parents, we can make a difference.

We can offer caring, acceptance and consistency, not only to our own children, but to all with whom we come in contact. For those children who don't have loving or nurturing parents, a teacher or neighbor may be the adult who brings warmth and dignity to their world. A little love and respect for the children who are starving for it can help emotionally maltreated children deal with their problems and, perhaps, even begin to teach them that they are valuable. It is my ardent hope that in such ways the vicious circle will be broken.

Notes

CHAPTER ONE

1. Miller, Alice, *For Your Good Good: Hidden Cruelty in Childrearing and the Roots of Violence,* tr. Hildegarde and Hunter Hannum. New York: Farrar, Straus & Giroux, 1983.

2. Kempe, C. Henry, "The Battered Child Syndrome," *Journal of the American Medical Association,* 181, 1962, pp. 17–24.

3. Miller, *op. cit.*

4. Gelles, Richard, "Child Abuse as Psychopathology," *American Journal of Orthopsychiatry,* 43, July, 1973, pp. 611–621.

5. Melnick, B. and Harley, J., "Distinctive Personality Attributes of Child-Abusing Mothers." *Journal of Consulting and Clinical Psychology,* 33, 1969, pp. 746–749.

6. Melnick, B. and Harley, J., *op. cit.*

7. Helfer, R. E., *et al.,* "Arresting or Freezing the Developmental Process," in R. E. Helfer, and C. H. Kempe, eds, *Child Abuse and Neglect: The Family and the Community,* Cambridge: Ballinger, 1976.

8. Pollack, C. B. and Steele, B. F., "A Therapeutic Approach to the Parents", in C. H. Kempe and R. E. Helfer, eds, *Helping the Battered Child and His Family,* Philadelphia: Lippincott, 1972.

9. Rohner, Ronald, *They Love Me, They Love Me Not,* New Haven: HRAF Press, 1975.

10. Hartley, S. F. *Illegitimacy,* Berkeley: University of California Press, 1975.

11. Simkin, L. "Consequences of Teenage Pregnancy and Motherhood," *Adolescence,* XIX, 73, 1984. pp.

12. Steele, B. F. and Pollack, C. B., "A Psychiatric Study of Parents Who Abuse Infants and Small Children," in R. E. Helfer and C. H. Kempe, eds., *The Battered Child,* 2nd edition, Chicago: University of Chicago Press, 1974, pp. 89–134.

13. Logan, Richard D., "Sociocultural Change and the Perception of Children as Burdens," *Child Abuse and Neglect,* 3, 1979, pp. 657–662.

14. Bettleheim, Bruno, "The Problem of Generations," in E. H. Erikson, ed., *The Challenge of Youth,* New York: Garden City, 1965.

15. Garbarino, James, "Defining Emotional Maltreatment: The Message is the Meaning," *Journal of Psychiatric Treatment and Evaluation,* Vol 2, 1980, pp. 105–110.

16. Miller, Alice, *Prisoners of Childhood,* tr. by Ruth Ward, New York: Basic Books, 1981.

17. Steele and Pollock, *op. cit.*

18. Scarf, Maggie, *Unfinished Business: Pressure Points in the Lives of Women,* New York: Ballantine Books, 1980.

19. Harlow, H. *et al.,* "The Maternal Affectional System of Rhesus Monkeys," in Reingold, H., (ed.) *Maternal Behavior in Mammals,* New York: Wiley, 1963.

Additional Bibliography

Aries, Philippe, *Centuries of Childhood: A Social History of Family Life,* tr. Robert Boldick, New York: Vintage Books, 1963.

Baldwin, W. and Cair, V. S., "The Children of Teenage Parents," in *Teenage Sexuality, Pregnancy, and Childbearing,* F. F. Furstenberg, et al., eds., Philadelphia: University of Pennsylvania Press, 1981.

Bolton, F. G., "Child Maltreatment Risk Among Adolescent Mothers," *American Journal of Orthopsychiatry,* 50, 1980, pp. 489–504.

Broman, S. H. "Long-Term Development of Children Born to Teenagers," in K. G. Scott, *et al.,* eds., *Teenage Parents and Their Offspring,* New York: Grune and Stratton, 1981.

Burgess, Robert L. and Conger, Rand D., "Family Interaction in Abusive, Neglectful and Normal Families," *Child Development,* 49, 1978, pp. 1163–1173.

DeMause, Lloyd, ed., *The History of Childhood,* New York: Psychohistory Press, 1974.

Elmer, Elizabeth, *Children in Jeopardy: A Study of Abused Minors and Their Families,* Pittsburgh: University of Pittsburgh Press, 1967.

Fontana, Vincent J. *Somewhere a Child Is Crying,* New York: MacMillan, 1973.

Fontana, Vincent J., "Which Parents Abuse Children?" in J. E. Leavitt, ed., *The Battered Child,* Fresno, California State University Press, 1974.

Radbill, S. X., "A History of Child Abuse and Infanticide," in R. E. Helfer and C. H. Kempe, eds., *The Battered Child,* Chicago: University of Chicago Press, 1968.

Straus, M. A., *et al., Behind Closed Doors: Violence in the American Family,* Garden City, N.Y.: Anchor/Doubleday, 1980.

Wasserman, Sidney, "The Abused Parent of the Abused Child," in J. E. Leavitt, ed. *The Battered Child,* Fresno: California State University Press, 1974.

CHAPTER TWO

1. Fraiberg, Selma, *Every Child's Birthright: In Defense of Mothering,* New York: Basic Books, 1977.

2. Klaus, Marshall H. and Kennell, John, *Maternal-Infant Bonding,* St. Louis: C. V. Mosby Co., 1976.

3. Parke, Ross D., "The Father of the Child," *The Sciences,* April 1979, pp. 12-15.

4. Erikson, Erik, *Childhood and Society,* New York: W. W. Norton Company, 1950.

5. Bowlby, John, *Attachment and Loss I: Attachment,* New York, Basic Books, 1969. *Attachment and Loss II: Separation Anxiety and Anger,* New York, Basic Books, 1973. *Attachment and Loss III: Sadness and Depression,* New York: Basic Books, 1980.

6. Fraiberg, Selma, *op. cit.*

7. Mahler, Margaret, "Rapprochement Subphase of the Separation/ Individuation Process," *Psychoanalytic Quarterly,* October 1972, pp. 487–506.

8. Reprinted with permission from Justin Call's work, "Child Abuse and Neglect in Infancy: Sources of Hostility Within the Parent-Infant Dyad and Disorders of Attachment in Infancy," in *Child Abuse and Neglect,* Volume 8, Elmsford, NY: Pergamon Press, © 1984, pp. 185–202.

Additional Bibliography

Brazelton, T. Berry, *et al.,* "The Origins of Reciprocity: the Early Mother-Infant Interaction," in M. Lewis and L. A. Rosenblum, eds., *The Effect of the Infant on the Caregiver,* Vol 1, New York: Wiley, 1974.

Egeland, Byron, and Sroufe, L. A., "Attachment and Early Maltreatment," *Child Development,* 52, 1981, pp. 44–52.

Dennis, Wayne, *Children of the Creche,* New York: Appleton, Century, Crofts, 1973.

Harlow, H. and Sumomi, S., "Induced Psychopathology in Monkeys," *Engineering and Science,* 33, 1970.

Lewis, M. and L. A. Rosenblum, eds., *The Effect of the Infant on the Caregiver,* Vol 1, New York: Wiley, 1974.

Lidz, Theodore, *The Person: His and Her Development Throughout the Life Cycle,* New York: Basic Books, 1976.

Pines, Maya, "Baby, You're Incredible," *Psychology Today,* Feb. 1982, pp. 48–53.

Scott, W. J., *Attachment and Child Abuse: A Study of Social History Indicators Among Mothers of Abused Children,* Ph.D. Dissertation, University of Minnesota, 1974.

Spitz, Rene, "Hospitalism: An Inquiry into the Genesis of Psychiatric Conditions in Early Childhood," *Psychoanalytic Study of the Child,* 1, 1945, pp. 53–74.

CHAPTER THREE

1. Goldstein, J., Freud, A., and Solnit, A., *Before the Best Interests of the Child,* New York: Free Press, 1979.

2. Armstrong, Louise, *The Home Front: Notes from the Family War Zone,* New York: McGraw Hill, 1983.

3. Miller, Alice, *For Your Own Good: Hidden Cruelty in Child Rearing and the Roots of Violence,* tr. Hildegarde and Hunter Hannum, New York: Farrar, Straus & Giroux, 1983.

4. Steele, B. F. and Pollack, C. B., "A Psychiatric Study of Parents Who Abuse Infants and Small Children," in Helfer, R. E. and Kempe, C. H., eds., *The Battered Child,* 2nd edition, Chicago: University of Chicago Press, 1974, pp. 89–134.

5. National Committee on Child Abuse and Neglect, 332 S. Michigan Avenue, Chicago, IL.

6. Garbarino, James, "Defining Emotional Maltreatment: The Message is the Meaning," *Journal of Psychiatric Treatment and Evaluation,* Vol 2, 1980, pp. 105–110.

7. Dean, Dorothy, "Emotional Abuse of Children," *Children Today,* July-August, 1979, pp. 18–20.

8. Yates, Alayne, "Legal Issues in Psychological Abuse of Children," *Clinical Pediatrics,* 21, no. 10, October, 1982.

9. Kaufman, I. R., (Chmn.) "Standards Relating to Abuse and Neglect, Recommended by the Institute on Judicial Administration-American Bar

Association Joint Committee on Juvenile Justice Standards," Cambridge: Ballinger Publishing Company, 1977, pp. 3–129.

10. American Humane Association, P.O. Box 1226, Denver, CO.

11. Garbarino, *op. cit.*

12. Kavanaugh, C., "Emotional Abuse and Mental Injury," *Journal of American Academy of Child Psychiatry,* 21, 1982, pp. 171–177.

Additional Bibliography

Dingwall, Robert and Eekelaar, John, "Social and Legal Perceptions of Child Neglect: Some Preliminary Considerations," *Child Abuse and Neglect,* 3, 1979, pp. 303–314.

Feshbach, N. D. and Feshbach, S., "Punishment: Parent Rites vs. Children's Rights," in Koocher, G. P. (ed.) *Children's Rights and the Mental Health Professions,* New York: Wiley, 1976.

Jayaratne, S., "Child Abusers as Parents and Children," *Social Work,* 22, 1977, pp. 5–9.

Lauer, James, "The Role of the Mental Health Professional in Child Abuse and Neglect," Manual distributed at the University of Colorado Child Abuse and Neglect Symposium, Keystone, Colorado, 1978.

Rosenheim, M. K., "The Child and the Law," in Grotberg, E. H., ed., *Two Hundred Years of Children,* Washington, D.C.: Office of Child Development, 1977.

Whiting, Leila, "Defining Emotional Neglect," *Children Today,* 5, 1976, pp. 2–5.

CHAPTER FOUR

1. Thomas, Alexander and Chess, Stella, "Genesis and Evolution of Behavioral Disorders: From Infancy to Early Adolescent Life," *American Journal of Psychiatry,* 141:1, January, 1984.

2. Chess, Stella and Thomas, Alexander, *Temperament and Behavior Disorders in Children,* New York: University Press, 1968.

3. Brazelton, T. Berry, *To Listen to A Child,* Reading, Mass: Addison-Wesley, 1984.

Additional Bibliography

Garmezy, N., and Rutter, M., eds., *Stress, Coping, and Development in Children,* New York: McGraw Hill, 1983.

CHAPTER FIVE

1. Briggs, Dorothy Corkille, *Your Child's Self Esteem: The Key To His Life,* Garden City, N.Y.: Doubleday, 1975.
2. Egeland, Byron, *et al.,* "The Developmental Consequence of Different Patterns of Maltreatment," *Child Abuse and Neglect,* 7, 1983, pp. 459–469.
3. Haynes, Clare, et al., "Hospitalized Cases of Non-Organic Failure to Thrive," *Child Abuse and Neglect,* 8, 1984, pp. 229–242.
4. Haynes, *op cit.*
5. Elkind, David, *The Hurried Child: Growing Up Too Fast Too Soon,* Reading, Mass: Addison-Wesley Publishing Company, 1981.
6. Winn, Marie, *Children Without Childhood,* New York: Penguin Books, 1981.
7. Garbarino, James, "The Elusive Crime of Emotional Abuse," *Child Abuse and Neglect,* 2, 1978, pp. 81–99.
8. Call, Justin, "Games Babies Play," *Psychology Today,* January, 1970, pp. 34–54.
9. Kennell, J. H., Klaus, M. H., et al., *Maternal-Infant Bonding,* St. Louis: C. V. Mosby Company, 1976.
10. Coopersmith, Stanley, *The Antecedents of Self-Esteem,* San Francisco: Freeman Publishing Company, 1967.

Additional Bibliography

Giblin, Paul T., *et al.,* "Affective Behavior of Abused and Control Children: Comparison of Parent-Child Interactions and the Influence of Home Environment Variables," *Journal of Genetic Psychology,* 144, 1984, pp. 69–82.

Haynes, Clare, *et al.,* "Non-Organic Failure-to-Thrive: Decisions for Placement and Videotaped Evaluations," *Child Abuse and Neglect,* 7, 1983, pp. 309–319.

Kennell, J. H. *et al.,* "Maternal Behavior One Year After Early and Extended Post-Partum Contact," *Developmental Medicine and Child Neurology,* 16, 1974, pp. 172–179.

Politt, E., *et al.,* "Psychosocial Development and Behavior of Mothers of Failure-to-Thrive Children," *American Journal of Orthopsychiatry,* 45, 1975, pp. 525–537.

Rosenberg, Mindy S. and Repucci, N. Dickon, "Abusive Mothers: Perception of Their Own and Their Children's Behavior," *Journal of Consulting and Clinical Psychology,* 51, 1983, pp. 674–682.

Wolfe, David A. and Mosk, Mark D., "Behavior Comparisons of Children from Abused and Distressed Families," *Journal of Consulting and Clinical Psychology,* 51, 1983, pp. 702–708.

CHAPTER SIX

1. Elkind, David, *The Hurried Child: Growing Up Too Fast Too Soon,* Reading, Mass: Addison-Wesley Publishing Company, 1981.

2. Winn, Marie, *Children Without Childhood,* New York: Penguin Books, 1981.

3. Postman, Neil, *The Disappearance of Childhood,* New York: Dell, 1984.

4. Marshner, Connaught, ed., *Family Protection Report,* Washington D.C.: Child and Family Protection Institute, February, 1984.

5. Long, Lynette and Thomas, *The Handbook for Latchkey Children and Their Parents,* New York: Berkley Books, 1984.

6. Dreskin, Wendy and William, *The Day Care Decision: What's Best for You and Your Child,* New York: Evans, 1983.

7. White, Burton, *The First Three Years of Life,* New York: Avon Books, 1975.

8. Dinnage, Rosemary, "Understanding Loss: The Bowlby Canon," *Psychology Today,* May, 1980, pp. 56–80.

Additional Bibliography

Working Mothers With Children, from the U.S. Dept. of Labor, Bureau of Labor Statistics, *Current Population Reports,* March, 1983

Weiss, Robert, "Growing Up a Little Faster: The Experience of Growing Up in a Single-Parent Household," *The Journal of Social Issues,* 35, 1979, p. 98.

CHAPTER SEVEN

1. Kinard, E. Milling, "Child Abuse and Depression: Cause or Consequence?" *Child Welfare,* Vol 61, No. 7, 1982, pp. 55–62.

2. Hopwood, Nancy and Becker, Dorothy, "Psychosocial Dwarfism: Detection, Evaluation, and Management", *Child Abuse and Neglect,* 3, 1979, pp. 439–447.

3. Gardner, L. I., "Deprivational Dwarfism," *Scientific American,* 1, 1977, p. 277.

4. Oates, R. Kim, "Similarities and Differences Between Non-Organic Failure-to-Thrive and Deprivational Dwarfism," *Child Abuse and Neglect,* 8, 1984, pp. 439–445.

5. Seligman, Martin, *Helplessness: On Depression, Development, and Death,* San Francisco: W. H. Freeman, 1975.

6. Rosenthal, Perihan and Rosenthal, Stuart, "Suicidal Behavior by Preschool Children," *American Journal of Psychiatry,* 141, 4, 1985, pp. 520–525.

7. Yates, Alayne, "Narcissistic Traits in Certain Abused Children," *American Journal of Orthopsychiatry,* 51, 1, January, 1981.

8. Egeland, Byron, et al., "The Developmental Consequences of Different Patterns of Maltreatment," *Child Abuse and Neglect,* 7, 1983, pp. 459–469.

9. Rohner, Ronald P. and Rohner, Evelyn, "Antecedents and Consequences of Parental Rejection," *Child Abuse and Neglect,* 4, 1980, pp. 189–198.

Additional Bibliography

Elmer, Elizabeth and Gregg, C. S., "Developmental Characteristics of Abused Children," *Pediatrics,* 40, 1967, pp. 596–612.

Green, A., "Psychopathology of Abused Children," *Journal of the American Academy of Child Psychiatry,* 17, 1978, pp. 92–103.

Martin, Harold P. and Rodeheffer, Martha, "Effects of Parental Abuse and Neglect on Children," *Journal of Pediatric Psychology,* 1, 1976, pp. 12–16.

Money, J. and Annecillo, C., "I.Q. Changes Following Change of Domicile in the Syndrome of Reversible Hyposomatotropinism," *Psychoneuroendocrinology,* 1, 1976, pp. 427–429.

Money, J., et al, "Pain agnosia and Self-Injury in the Syndrome of Reversible Somatotropic Deficiency," *Journal Autism and Child Schizophrenia,* 2, 1972, pp. 127–139.

Money, J. and Needleman, A., "Child Abuse in the Syndrome of Reversible Hyposomatotropinism," *Pediatric Psychology,* 1, 1976, pp. 20–23.

Patton, R. G., and Garner, L. I., "Deprivational Dwarfism: Disordered Family Environment as Cause of So-called Idiopathic Hypopiuitarism," in Gardner, L. I., ed., *Endocrine and Genetic Diseases of Childhood and Adolescence,* (Vol 2) Philadelphia: L. B. Saunders, 1975.

Sassin, J. F., et al, "Human Growth Hormone Release: Relation to Slow-Wave Sleep and Sleep-Waking Cycles," *Science,* 165, 1967, pp. 513–515.

Schneider-Rosen, Karen, and Cicchetti, Dante, "Relationship Between Affect and Cognition in Maltreated Infants," *Child Development,* 55, 1984, pp. 648–658.

Seligman, Martin, "Fall into Helplessness," *Psychology Today,* June, 1973.

Sroufe, L. A. "Attachment and the Roots of Competence," *Human Nature,* October 1978, pp. 1050–1059.

CHAPTER EIGHT

1. Anthony, E. J., "The Syndrome of the Psychologically Invulnerable Child," in Anthony, E. J. and Koupernik, C., eds., *The Child In His Family: Children at Psychiatric Risk,* New York: Wiley, 1974.

2. Rutter, Michael, "Protective Factors in Children's Response to Stress and Disadvantage," in Kent, M. W. and Rolfe, J. E., eds., *Primary Prevention of Psychopathology and Social Competence in Children,* Vol. 3, Hanover, N.H.: University Press of New England, 1974.

3. Heider, G. M., "Vulnerability in Infants and Young Children," *Genetic Psychology Monograph,* 73, 1966, pp. 1–216.

4. Rutter, Michael, "Sex Differences in Children's Responses to Family Stress," in Anthony, E. J. and Koupernik, C., eds., *The Child in His Family: Children at Psychiatric Risk,* Vol. 3, New York: Wiley, 1970.

5. Anthony, E. J., *op. cit.*

6. Pines, Maya, "Resilient Children," *Psychology Today,* March, 1984, pp. 57–85.

7. Garmezy, Norman, "Children Under Stress: Perspectives on Antecedents and Correlates of Vulnerability and Resistance to Psychopathology," in Rabin, A. I., *et al.,* eds., *Further Explorations in Personality,* New York: Wiley, 1981.

8. Rutter, Michael, *et al.,* eds., *Fifteen Thousand Hours: Secondary Schools and Their Effects on Children,* Cambridge: Harvard University Press, 1979.

Additional Bibliography

Anthony, E. J., "A New Scientific Region to Explore," in Anthony, E. J. and Koupernik, C., eds., *The Child In His Family: Children at Psychiatric Risk,* New York, Wiley, 1978.

Rutter, Michael and Garmezy, N., eds., *Stress, Coping, and Development in Children,* New York: McGraw Hill, 1983.

CHAPTER NINE

1. Krugman, Richard D. and Mary K., "Emotional Abuse in the Classroom: The Pediatrician's Role in Diagnosis and Treatment", *American Journal of Diseases of Children,* 138, March, 1984, pp. 284–289.

2. Krugman, *op cit.*

3. Campbell-Smith, Mollie, "The School: Liberator or Censurer?" *Child Abuse and Neglect,* 7, 1983, pp. 329–337.

4. Rutter, Michael, *et al.,* eds., *Fifteen Thousand Hours: Secondary Schools and Their Effects on Children,* Cambridge: Harvard University Press, 1978.

5. Wolfe, S., *Children Under Stress,* Baltimore: Penguin Books, 1973.

6. Rosenthal, Robert, "The Pygmalion Effect Lives," *Psychology Today,* September 1973, pp. 56–63.

Additional Bibliography

Clarizo, Harvey F., *Toward Positive Classroom Discipline,* New York: Wiley, 1976.

Gil, David G., "What Schools Can Do About Child Abuse," in Leavitt, James E., ed., *The Battered Child,* Fresno: California State University Press, 1974.

Hyman, Irwin A. and D'Alessandro, "Good Old-Fashioned Discipline: The Politics of Punitiveness," *Phi Delta Kappan,* September 1984, pp. 39–45.

CHAPTER TEN

1. Quote attributed. For further study, see: Menninger, Karl, *Crime of Punishment,* New York: Viking Press, 1968.

2. Bronfenbrenner, Urie, "Who Needs Parent Education?" *Teachers College Record,* 79, 1978, pp. 767–787.

3. Bellah, Robert, *Habits of the Heart,* Berkeley: University of California Press, 1985.

4. Helfer, R. E., *Childhood Comes First,* E. Lansing, Michigan: Author, 1978.

5. Behavior Associates, *Parents Anonymous Self-Help for Child-Abusing Parents Project: Evaluation Report,* Tucson: Behavior Associates, 1977.

6. Garbarino, James, "The Elusive Crime of Emotional Abuse," *Child Abuse and Neglect,* 2, 1978, pp. 81–99.

7. Gottlieb, Benjamin, H., "The Role of Individual and Social Support in Preventing Child Maltreatment," in Garbarino, James and Stocking, S. Holly, eds., *Protecting Children from Abuse and Neglect,* San Francisco: Jossey-Bass, 1980.

8. Reprinted with permission from "Evaluating Child Abuse Prevention Programs" (pp. v–vi), by Ellen Gray and Joan DiLeonardi, © 1982, by permission of the publisher, The National Committee for Prevention of Child Abuse, 332 S. Michigan Avenue, Chicago: 1982.

9. Rohner, Ronald P. and Evelyn C., "Antecedents and Consequences of Parental Rejection: A Theory of Emotional Abuse," *Child Abuse and Neglect,* 4, 1980, pp. 189–198.

10. Bolton, Frank G., Jr., "From Theory to Practice," in *When Bonding Fails: Clinical Assessment of High Risk Families,* Beverly Hills: Sage Publications, 1983.

Additional Bibliography

Beezley, P., *et al,* "Comprehensive Family-Oriented Therapy," in Helfer, R. E. and Kempe, C. H., eds., *Child Abuse and Neglect: The Family and Community,* Cambridge: Ballinger, 1976.

Cohn, A. H., *et al,* "Evaluating Innovative Treatment Programs," Children Today, 4, 1975, pp. 10–12.

Escalona, Sybille, "Intervention Programs for Children at Psychiatric Risk," in Anthony, E. J. and Koupernik, C., eds., *The Child in His Family: Children at Psychiatric Risk,* New York: Wiley, 1974

Jeffry, Margaret, "Practical Ways to Change Parent-Child Interaction in Families of Children at Risk," in *Child Abuse and Neglect,* Helfer, R. E. and C. H. Kempe, eds., Cambridge: Ballinger, 1976.

Katz, Sanford, *When Parents Fail: The Law's Response to Family Breakdown,* Boston: Beacon Press, 1971.

CHAPTER ELEVEN

1. Gordon, Thomas, *Parent Effectiveness Training: The Tested New Way to Raise Responsible Children,* New York, McKay, 1970.

2. Ascher, B. L., "Son Worship," *Redbook,* July 1983, Vol. 161, p. 174.

3. Briggs, Dorothy Corkille, *Your Child's Self-Esteem,* Garden City, N.Y.: Doubleday, 1975.

Additional Bibliography

Chess, Stella; Thomas, Alexander; and Brich, Herbert, *Your Child Is a Person: A Psychological Approach to Parenthood Without Guilt,* New York: Penguin Books, 1965.

Cousins, Norman, *Anatomy of an Illness As Perceived by the Patient,* New York, Bantam, 1981.

Lickona, Thomas, *Raising Good Children,* New York: Bantam Books, 1983.

CHAPTER TWELVE

1. Miller, William, *Make Friends With Your Shadow: How to Accept and Use Positively the Negative Side of Your Personality,* Minneapolis: Augsburg Publishing House, 1981.

Additional Bibliography

Menninger, Karl, *The Vital Balance: The Life Process in Mental Health and Illness,* New York: Viking, 1963.

Missildine, W. Hugh, *Your Inner Child of the Past,* New York: Simon and Schuster, 1963.

Powell, John, *Fully Human, Fully Alive,* Niles, Ill: Argus Press, 1976.

Satir, Virginia, *Peoplemaking,* Palo Alto: Science and Behavior Books, 1972.